MANIFESTOS FOR THE 21ST CENTURY

SERIES EDITORS: URSULA OWEN AND JUDITH VIDAL-HALL

Free expression is as high on agenda as it has ever been, though not always for the happiest of reasons. Here, distinguished writers address the issue of censorship in a complex and fragile world where people with widely different cultural habits and beliefs are living in close proximity, where offence is easily taken, and where words, images and behaviour are coming under the closest scrutiny. These books will surprise, clarify and provoke in equal measure.

ASYLUM AND EXILE

The Hidden Voices of London

BIDISHA

LONDON NEW YORK CALCUTTA

Seagull Books, 2014

© Bidisha, 2014

ISBN 978 0 8574 2 210 1

British Library Cataloguing-in-Publication Data
A catalogue record for this book is available from the British Library.

Typeset in Minion Pro and Corbel by Seagull Books, Calcutta, India
Printed and bound by Hyam Enterprises, Calcutta, India

For Beatrice Tibahurira

CONTENTS

ACKNOWLEDGEMENTS

This book was inspired by a residency with English PEN, the literature and human rights organization. The project, 'Big Writing for a Small World', was funded by the European Commission Representation in the United Kingdom as part of its intention to 'support social inclusion and combat discrimination' and was undertaken between late 2011 and mid 2012.

There are many ongoing academic studies, grassroots initiatives, activist campaigns, research projects and commissioned reports on migration, asylum and refugees. But there are also several books which provide an excellent combination of history, policy and context for lay readers. They helped me enormously when it came to developing a background understanding of my students' experiences. These books are listed in the bibliography of this volume.

During the writing of this book, I kept up to date with new developments, campaigns and research surrounding issues of migration, asylum, human rights and refugees by following the work of many charities, in particular Women For Refugee Women, Women Asylum Seekers Together, the Paul Hamlyn Foundation, the Helen Bamber Foundation, the International Rescue Committee and Asylum Aid.

Sincere thanks go to the wonderful, talented and indefatigable Philip Cowell, formerly of English PEN, for offering me what turned out to be a life-changing and humbling opportunity. Thanks also to Polly for great intelligence and tact under pressure.

I want to express my solidarity with and admiration for the other writers involved in the project, teaching elsewhere in the UK: Shazea Quraishi, Malika Booker, Nii Parkes, Seni Seneviratne, Degna Stone, Maeve Clarke, Tania Hershman and John Siddique. Thanks to everyone at Praxis in Bethnal Green, London, especially Bethan Lant for her commitment, expertise, knowledge and tenacity. Thanks to the Migrants Resource Centre in Victoria, London, especially Laura Marziale, for dedication, aptitude and smart thinking. Thanks, as always, to Seagull Books and the University of Chicago Press, in particular my publisher Naveen Kishore and editors Ursula Owen and Judith Vidal-Hall.

My greatest thanks, however, go to my students, some of whose names I have changed for discretion. I hope their intelligence, talent and vivacity come through in these pages and that together we achieved the project's goals, which were—in the words of English PEN—to raise the profile of literature as a means of combating social exclusion, to give a platform to unheard voices from marginalized communities and to get settling and existing UK communities to share stories, memories and reflections.

And thank you, first and last, to Beatrice Tibahurira, whose name and words I haven't changed, who gave me permission to feature her work and who I know will go on to be a much-loved author.

CHAPTER ONE

NO MORE LIES

'They put electricity through me. You know electricity?' The Kurdish Iraqi man shows me how Saddam Hussein's men electrocuted him. 'And . . .'

He gestures again, lashing his forearm.

'They whipped you, with electrical cord,' I say. 'And your family?'

'They killed my mother, my sisters.'

'Do you ever think about them? The people who did it.'

'No. I never think about them. I came here to Bethnal Green. The first week, burgled. They took everything, including the bedsheets and the light bulbs.'

A wry smile. As we finish the interview he asks me, with rough-edged chivalry, 'Is there anything I can do for you?'

That was seven years ago at an East London resource centre for asylum seekers, refugees and displaced people. I was writing an article about the area's migrants, outreach projects, youth groups, homeless people and community leaders and had discovered a secret slice of the city: thousands of individuals from hundreds of countries, people who were not hipsters or bankers, who weren't thriving or on the make but in some cases barely surviving. They had fallen between the cracks and were stereotyped, stigmatized, exploited and overlooked, yet determined to make a life. Articles were written about them—scare stories, moralizing stories, sob stories—but their own voices were rarely heard. When I handed the article in, the editor wasn't convinced. The story was too grimy and unglamorous, not swinging or aspirational enough. The piece was killed and the voices died with it.

Seven years later I return to the same centre, to teach. The place is built into and around a cottagey church just off the main road in Bethnal Green. The rough church stone is soaked with rain. As I cross the road, a white truck goes past with the words No More Lies traced into the dirt on its side. Outside the main door there's a rickety-looking homeless guy on crutches, a skinny roll-up pinched in his crooked fingers, wet plastic bags at his feet. I glance over him as he squints against the cigarette smoke. *A Place for the Displaced*, says a sign by the door.

Inside, the entrance room has a mood of chummy stoicism. There's a multiracial mishmash of people in winter coats sitting stiffly on plastic chairs and there are posters pinned to the walls giving phone numbers for hotlines and services for legal advice, English classes, basic-skills qualifications, professional training and music workshops. One young man shows another young man his wedding photographs; both are grinning bashfully. The grille of the cafe is up and they're serving cheaply priced tea and cakes. I check what's for lunch: an Indian fish dish and an African stew. My kind of people.

I sit down for a second and a little boy in a puffa jacket comes up, chattering and pointing to my lap.

'Hello, sunshine face,' I say.

'He's speaking to you in his language,' smiles his mother.

The classroom's at the end of a long, thin corridor lined with pictures of local community choirs and singing groups. The wooden-floored church hall on the left smells warmly of violin-bow rosin and there are two tall, gentle-bellied African drums up on the dais. On the right are scruffy, nearly bare meeting rooms with starchy dark carpet tiles, schoolroom desks and buzzing fluorescent lighting.

The class was meant to have begun five minutes ago but the room's empty. It's big, fit for a group of 30, with heavy, stackable classroom furniture, but dingy and unheated. The floor's marked with sooty black smears. Eventually, the people who'd been in the waiting room amble in, greet me, desultorily reach for a piece of paper, take a pen, have a chat, check their phone, skiddle the pen across the paper and look at me, flatly friendly. Both sexes, all ages from 20 to 70, the majority from African countries, with the exception of a dusky, skinny, smiling man as tall as a lamp post, with thick glasses, in a limp black suit, gazing around with soft delight. He looks like a cartoon undertaker.

I explain that I'm doing a residency with a charity specializing in—

'You say you're from a charity. So give us some money,' interrupts a man on my left.

He's in his 60s, chubby and stocky, looking up at me with an impish, challenging smile.

'Not *that* kind of charity. A *literary* charity,' I say. 'What's your name?'

'Don. Well—Dimbi, for the purposes of immigration and legal matters. But here everyone calls me Don.'

'I think I need to learn who everyone is. Could you go round and write down your name and age and where you're from . . . not if you don't want to . . . and the languages you speak and the number of years you've been in the UK? Not for immigration purposes, I promise. I just want to know a bit about you.'

'Don't ask. You'll have nightmares,' says Don, and the rest of the class agrees. 'Write something down,' he orders, pointing to the whiteboard.

I notice as I squeak across the board that Don doesn't write anything down himself. Actually, very few of them do. Don tells me he was born in 1964, has been here since 1997 and speaks Lingala and French. He tells me his favourite person is 'Teacher' and I scoff while he grins.

Next to Don is a man in his 40s with an oval face and large, cold, heavy brown eyes. He too doesn't bother writing anything. I see him looking around the classroom, first at all the women and then, rather calculatingly, at everyone in general. His name's Claude.

'When I'm asked what is my home, I say Planet Earth,' he says. 'Since I left my country, in Congo, what home is there? No home. I am in limbo, a travelling man. I am like a yoyo. A bachelor. You hear that? I am looking for a wife. Since I came to this country, if I had a child then, that child

would be 11 years old by now. And I still don't have indefinite leave to stay.'

'You're going to have nightmares now,' Don cuts in,
nodding to me.

'I am here for 11 years,' Claude goes on, 'I have my
meeting at the Home Office where a 19-year-old girl who
doesn't know anything about anything, asking stupid questions, says, "Everything you have said is just a story you
made up."'

As he says the words 'just a story you made up', the rest
of the class chimes in and laughs.

'They do not believe us,' states Claude, and the class
nods.

My students are living in the UK but most have not
been granted indefinite leave to stay and do not have the
right to work or access public funds. When they do work,
it's off the books: cleaning, caring, maintenance work, factory work, building work, menial work.

Don says to me, 'I do odd cleaning jobs. It's OK.' He
shrugs. 'I was in detention for five months. In a detention
centre. And then, with a tag—an electronic tag.'

'Which centre? Oh . . . Campsfield House? Swansea?
I've been in that one . . .' the others call out.

'Let me tell you! I will tell you,' cries a lively and beautiful Cameroonian woman named Banyina sitting smack
bang in the middle of the row and occasionally jiving in her
seat to an unheard tune. She has a suitably beautiful real
name which she says means 'the way is always open to me.

There is no obstacle. I can do anything.' She speaks English and French and she has been in the UK since 2004. She's 34. She tells me, 'I have been working since I got here, working in a company. I got my NVQ in Business Management. I was the only black in the company. I was a manager,' she says proudly. 'And then a friend of mine, she wanted to work for that company also. I said, "Apply, but I don't want to interview you in case they say, oh, you know, 'She chose her because they're both black . . .' " Anyway, one day, the police show up. I don't know who called them. They show up. They know my name. They have a photograph of me. They say, "Oh, you are here illegally." Because there was some issue with the details of my application form. They take me there from my place of work! In front of everyone—oh!' She clutches her head. 'And they arrest me. They kept me there for three days in a cell. I had nothing. I wasn't allowed to take a shower, I wasn't allowed to wash and I'll tell you, I was menstruating so badly. They said, "She is really smelling bad." I shouted at them to let me take a shower. I shouted, "You have mothers, you have sisters, you have daughters, you have girlfriends. Would you treat them like this?" Finally they let me. I went to court. I went to a prison. I went to a detention centre.'

The stories pour out, so fast that if I urge them to write some of them down they shake their heads impatiently and carry on talking. Many of the class have had similar experiences, supporting what I've been reading in a piece by Jerome Phelps, the director of Detention Action, in the newspaper *Migrant Voice*. Phelps writes that 'only migrants can be locked up without time limit, for no crime, and without automatic review by the courts. Most migrants who are detained have committed no crime; none are serving a criminal sentence; they lose their liberty simply because of their immigration status.'[1] He cites a man named Sami, a builder and gardener who was put in four different detention centres for more than a year after fleeing persecution in his own country. In one centre he witnessed the death of another detainee, who was ill and asking for help, after staff refused to get a doctor.

New students are coming in at their leisure, even half an hour into the session. The door opens and in stumps the guy on crutches, shoulders hunched. He goes to the far corner where two equally shady skinny men gladly make space, clapping him on the back. He soon picks up the flavour of the conversation, waving his arms about, looking directly at me and ignoring the pen and paper in front of him.

'I'll tell you something that happened to me. I won't write it down, I'll tell you. I was on the street. You know. Smoking.' He pronounces it 'smocking' and mimes a tight, pleasurable puff on a thin cigarette. 'And I turn and I saw a man—he was being beaten up! Beaten up. He was on the ground, beaten up, and the man who was kicking him had metal on his boots. You know, metal, on the boots?'

'You saw a man being kicked by a guy who had steel toecaps on his boots?' I say.

1 Jerome Phelps, 'Banged Up for No Crime, with No Time-Limit', *Migrant Voice* 1 (2012): 28. Available at: http://migrantforum.org.uk/wp-content/-uploads/full-MV-paper.pdf (last accessed on 4 January 2014).

'Yes! And the man, he ran away, and the other man is lying, beaten up. I call the police. I go to the man to, you know, to help him. And the police come—and they arrest me! They arrest *me*.'

Everyone's listening and tutting and shaking their heads and nodding their heads and frowning and saying, 'Mm-hmm.'

'Outrageous. Outrageous!' I say.

'Yes. They arrest me, they put on their gloves, latex gloves. "What's in here?" They open my bag where I have all my, you know, my bits and pieces, camera, diary, wallet with £480. They took it. It took me three months to get it all back. They took me. Put me in a cell for three nights. Even though I was the one helping. Then eventually, another guy, who saw what had happened, went in and said, "No, it wasn't him."'

'Did the guy who did it get caught?'

'He didn't even bother to turn up at the police station.'

'Did you get all your stuff back off the police?'

'Yes. Oh yes.'

He leans back in his chair, nodding, steaming slightly with indignation. Half the session has passed. At break time, there's a big rush as a staff member wheels a sturdy wooden trolley down the ramp and offers tea and spongy cakes to everyone. A centre volunteer who's studying social work comes in and gives us a knackered-looking little fan heater. We point it so that it heats the ankles of as many of us as possible. Claude is assiduously getting tea for the ladies, addressing the older women as 'Auntie' and being most expressive with the younger ones, who give him very short shrift.

Everyone's put their empty mug back on the trolley apart from the shady guys in the corner. A woman who'd been loudly rejecting Claude gets up and tells them off as she takes their mugs.

'Who do you think is gonna do that? Who is gonna pick up your mug?' To me she shakes her head and says, 'Men! They will not do the work.'

When we've settled down again I plead with them to write me two lines of the simplest exercises possible: A Happy Memory; My Favourite Thing; A Letter. Some of them indulge me but Claude, Don and a few others blink, look around and do nothing. Some of the students seem small and cowed, crumpled over in their seats, frowning when I talk too fast. Everyone's still wearing their coat and scarf.

'Where do you live?' Don asks me.

I tell him.

'What bus number is that? Is it the 22? No—the 27?'

'From here? I just get the Tube,' I say, puzzled, while the students compare bus routes and times and compete over their transport-network knowledge.

With a prickle of embarrassment, I realize that the bus is cheaper than the Tube. My students mostly live in far Greater London; the journey into town takes well over an hour. I can tell by their conversations that it's standard to walk for however long it takes to a particular bus stop so that they'll then only need to take one bus rather than change.

When the first exercises are handed in, I look over them and try quickly to memorize names and details. I learn that one of the shady guys in the corner, streetwise, fit and lively, with a broad London accent, is 36 and has 5 brothers and 2 sisters. He's originally from Malawi but has been in the UK for 13 years and is pretty established here. He speaks English, Swahili, Chewa, Tumbuka and 'broken French' and his favourite person, he writes, is 'Bill Clinton, for doing so much for Africa and black people in general.'

There's a woman on my right with a soft, receiving face and a mournful mouth. She's large, reticent and solid, one of the older students in the class. She has a library book with her, a memoir by a Middle Eastern woman. Whenever she talks, everyone else goes silent and listens, without realizing they're doing it. She's composed a few lines about herself in clear, elegant writing. Her name is Beatrice Tibahurira and she's in her late 50s, although she looks older.

She writes:

> My hobby has always been reading books. Ever since I learnt how to read, I've read all sorts of books. I have read novels, history books, magazines. My life in the UK hasn't been easy but what I would like now most is to regularise my stay so I can freely work or maybe write more. I feel I have so much in my head that I would like to put into written form.

I was born in the south western part of Uganda on the 6th of January 1956. The town in which I was born is called Kabale. It was a small town then. Now it has grown into a big business city as it's on the routes out of Uganda to both Congo and Rwanda. In my childhood, my friends and relatives called me Bea, short for Beatrice. Some of them still do now.

Beatrice has 5 brothers and 6 sisters and lived first in Kabale and then in Kampala. She's been in the UK for 10 years and has lived as an asylum seeker in London, Cornwall and Bristol, among other places. She speaks Runyakitala, Luganda and English.

She clears her throat and in a clear, deep, calm voice reads out, 'I saw my son when he was 9 and then saw him again at 15 and a half. He was a man. I saw him standing next to his sister and I thought he was a neighbour, or a friend. My daughter said, "This is Maurice." Well, I fell down, fainting, crying. Tears of joy.'

'And now?' I ask.

'He is a real man. Studying at Southampton University.'

'Well done him. You write so well.'

'Yes. I want to write. We've been through so much—and so much has happened along the way—good things and bad.'

Sitting alertly at the corner of the table is a stylish woman with a hard and steely glint in her eye. Her hand goes up every time I ask a question and she mutters to herself as she writes. I heard her earlier refusing a cake with the words, 'What's in that? No. I don't eat sugar.' She's volunteered to teach sewing and design classes here. Her name's Jeanne Longomba and she's from the Democratic Republic of Congo. She's been in the UK for '10 years and 2 months,' she writes, and speaks Kinande, Swahili, Lingala and English. She's done previous writing courses here and wasn't going to be let on to this one because it's for new people, until she kicked up a fuss. She points to some of the people in the room and tells them off for 'laughing when I was crying. It is very rude to do that, you know.'

Well, Jeanne may be rebarbative but maybe that's what you need to survive, and she writes like a dream:

> In my early teenage years I loved having my school holidays with my cousins in Butembo. The journey was full of beautiful scenery: the snowy mountain ranges that kept on getting closer and closer as the bus crossed to the southern part of Virunga National Park, the scattered savannah trees that seemed like they were moving as we drove faster. The bus was driven under the hot sun of Africa in the Democratic Republic of Congo. I loved seeing herds of animals like buffaloes mixed with antelopes, elephants grazing on the fresh green grass and giraffe leaping to feed themselves on the savannah trees.
>
> I have lived far away from my siblings for ten years. Sorrow strikes me when I realise I am growing on my own, without them. What I miss so much is the time my parents collected us together

to have dinner when we lived at Katwa-Butembo in DR Congo. Then I remember my dad and mum would read Bible stories. I remember also that we ran to school so that we were not late. I remember my lovely sister who was ten years older than me held my hand and told me to run as fast as she did, but I could not, as I was young and the seventh child out of nine. I remember running very very much trying to keep her pace, but it was all very tiring. I remember the beautiful uniform my dad used to sew for me. I remember going with my mother to the market which was full of so many lovely items to eat, especially the harvested passion fruits.

The rest of the class ignores Jeanne's vigorous, clever, detailed prose. She tells me about how she's been treated in the UK. She hasn't been detained or imprisoned as some of her classmates have but has been moved around the country, always in temporary accommodation, in shared houses grouped by ethnicity, religion, country—a tenuous, subjugated, crudely demarcated and unstable life in which she has no say over anything. In her last piece of writing she states firmly, 'I now want the Home Office to consider my status so that I can create more and more to serve everyone in communities. I want to have my own accommodation. I want the UK government to know that I would like to stay in England to serve.'

CHAPTER TWO

WHY IS LIFE SO DODGY?

After the first lesson, I go to the Museum of Childhood to write my notes. The museum's exhibits are kitschily macabre and campily beautiful, an Angela Carter story brought to life, all wax dolls, tin automata and ivory rocking horses. I count 20 adults in the ground-floor cafe, all white except for me, nearly all women, all but a few with children. They may not be rich but they're rich enough, and comfortable in these surroundings. They have colourful, well-made, stylish clothes and good buggies. My students have disappeared, gone for appointments, to do work or training or take more classes or go on long bus journeys elsewhere.

I look through the school exercise books I'd given out. Many are empty but for a name on the front or a scratch of ink in the corner. There are some students who've left a few lines about themselves but don't return to the group: Ramula Wanyana, 33 years old, has been here for 13 years, speaks English and Luganda and has 1 brother and 3 sisters; Glorianna N'Yaleima Cole, 35, from Sierra Leone, has been here for 5 years, speaks English, Creole and Wlende and has 2 brothers and 3 sisters.

What little writing I find is in broken or phonetic English, or English transliterated from French. A woman named Cecile Weta writes, 'Death is destruction for many families. My husband death, my life change and I have a bad life!' A woman named Julienne writes, 'Example my brother daid 2003, I filling very sad because he was good men.' A woman named Seida Ndoloma writes, 'I lose everything I wanted to build, it's like I build in vain.'

The following piece is anonymous:

The end of life.
Death is separation, painful.
My father's death 2003, I no like because my father is good parent for me.
My sister death 1993, make big problem for my mum. Mum is not survive death from my sister.
In my country, in certain cities, a lot of women die because the rebels rape and they can not survive it.

The smiling, tall, skinny man in the suit has handwriting like a four-year-old: big, square, gappy and hard-cornered, with a full inch between each line, sliding off the page from the top left to the bottom right. He writes that his name is Manny, he's 51 and from Iran. So, he's getting to grips with a different alphabet altogether. He writes, 'I don't know many people. My landlord's office and my partner's in a music band. These people know me honest and cool. Kind and hard worker in music.'

At the next lesson there he is, a magical daddy-long-legs, watching and smiling and twitching gently.

'Manny,' I say. 'You said you work in music. What did you mean?'

'I am a musician.' He has a high, airy, twittering voice, sibilant and sad, like a dying tin whistle.

'What kind of music?'

'Persian kind.'

'Persian classical? You mean . . . you play it . . . and I think you teach it?'

Manny nods, his crossed wrists on his crossed knees, the toe of his skinny, black leather shoe pointing up to the ceiling.

'I was a teacher in a university. Many, many students.'

'And then?'

'When I left Iran, I went to France. And there—Persian music. Yes, yes. They do classes. There are people. But here, no Persian music. You can't do.'

I try to cajole him into doing some written work to improve his English and he laughs it off gaily but does submit a nice one-liner about the sun: 'Sun, when we are tired from darkness you will come.' I'd given everyone the challenge of writing something about the sun that doesn't involve any clichés. On the board, I draw a sun with a smiling face and rays and all its clichés flowing out from it: warmth, light, shininess, redness, yellowness and gold, nourishment, hope and life and growth, tanning and health, sunset and sunrise. These are all banned.

A woman with a canny face, gleaming jet skin and matte black eyes chuckles as she prepares to read hers out. Grandly, emphatically: 'I miss the African sun because it made me sweat out all my African fat.'

Clapping, laughter and loud agreement from everyone.

'You're coming back next week, we've got a funny one here!' I say.

A warm, big, trendy young woman named Elodie, from the Congo, reads out something that sounds fluent and natural. She has a French-inflected Cockney accent and an air of sloppy, lazy likeableness. At the end of the first lesson she had asked me, with a flashing smile, 'I really like your pen. Can I have it?'

'Oh, whatever you can get for free, is it?' I grumbled, giving it to her.

Elodie is 31, has been in the UK for 8 years and lived in Stoke on Trent, Leytonstone and Birmingham. She tells me she speaks 'perfect French, Lingala and bad English'. Looking through her written work, I realize that so many students are getting along conversationally, aided by their personality and charisma, but need to sharpen the precision of their written English. Elodie writes to the sun, 'When you shine you make me fil that I am inlive. You give me hope, gide me and when I sow you apperence shining it mint for me that you are always with me and you are good. Friend, you are like a shadow who walk with me all the time.' Her favourite place is 'A place I will learn new thinks and devellope my knolege because I love challenge. And also I am doing travel and tourism now so I love to be where I will learning exciting thinks.'

I like the idea of learning 'exciting thinks'. This is exactly what my students are doing for me—showing me a new way of looking at the world and a new way of thinking about it. I can say with my hand on my heart that I wield no authority over them whatsoever. I can barely get them to pick up a pen, let alone edit a sentence—though speaking of pens, the calm woman, Beatrice, tells me hers is her favourite thing, 'I go everywhere with it. It is as if it is a part of me.'

Talk turns to landscape and Manny wants to tell me about one of his nicest memories. He starts swooping his pen over the paper. I get pleased because I think he's doing some writing, but no, he's drawing me a map.

'It happen in the south of Iran . . . here the sea . . . I was soldier.'

'*You* were a soldier?'

'Yes,' he says, with uncharacteristic grimness, and I shut up.

He shows me the coast on his map. Instead of writing, he recites:

'I was walking there—I was a soldier.

Really it was a beautiful sea.

It was early morning when the sun was coming up—so many colours.

At night the sea is quiet, no waves, without moving.

I felt I could walk on the surface of the sea.'

Meanwhile Claude—who I have nicknamed Mr Loverman because of his antics—can't be doing with all this talk of seas and sunrises and wants to get down to basics. He says his ideal situation would be 'a bigamist family with a huge number of kids, 5 mums with 32 kids!' We all groan and reprove him. Later, though, I find that he's filled a few pages of his exercise book. It's surprising after his extreme reticence during the first few sessions and his portrayal of himself as a breezily predatory cad with nothing to hide and nothing to lose. We had been looking at various In Memoriam poems and elegies earlier and he's written to his mother: 'Your name is Celeste, forever . . . I cry and cry, no answer for my consolation, the tears of a crocodile inside the water . . . in heaven you have a bouquet of flowers from my lonely heart.'

And there is also a poem by him, called 'Divorce':

I saw you one day under heavenly rain,
Your look was so beautiful and exciting,
The way you talked was as the ocean's wave.
I was so shocked, the smell of your perfume when
you started talking,
Your body language was so sexy that I decided to
get you as a part of my life.
Marriage was the only way to show the huge love
to you!
I didn't know that the black moment would come.
Why is life so dodgy?
The one I love and put a diamond ring on
Brought me to the Judge for a divorce.
She accused me of all kinds of sins of this world.
Is the divorce a part of love?
Is love a part of divorce?
Could I celebrate my divorce as I did my marriage?

In the classroom I keep things light, simple, even trivial. Yet every prompt, no matter how banal, cracks open great depths. I notice how many of my students, when asked about their favourite thing, tell me it's their phone. One says, 'It's nothing special. It doesn't show videos. It can't take pictures. But it means I can speak to people.' This echoes something a staff member at the centre told me in a briefing meeting months ago: 'The phone is essential if you don't know what's going on and you need to link up all the different parts of your life. It's a lifeline, it's their survival.'

There is a quiet, nice, slightly fragile-seeming woman in her early 60s in the class, who speaks and writes impeccably but who always comes to me worrying about the quality of her English. Her name's Rose Brenya and she's one of 7 children—she has 3 brothers and 3 sisters—from Ghana. She's lived in the UK for 15 years, currently in a convent house in Surrey, and speaks English, Ghanaian and Achi. When we were talking about landscapes earlier, she said, 'I like forests because my parents were farmers. We used to go there every Saturday to find food and other things and plant yams, plantains and cocoyam.'

'Can you do an exercise where you tell me how to write something perfectly?' she asks me during break one day, her voice trembling.

'Yes, of course I can, but you can also show me anything you've got and I'll mark it. And you know, you already speak and write perfectly.'

She looks pained and shakes her head. Tears spring to her eyes.

'No, no, that is what everyone says. But I want to *know . . .*'

'Your only problem is confidence. You have to speak. You're not speaking!'

In the class she gently pulls up her coat sleeve and shows us her wrist.

'My favourite thing is my gold watch. I like it because it was given to me by all my children when I became 60.'

We all coo at this nice gesture.

'How many kids've you got?' I ask.

'Six. And 12 grandchildren.'

With a smart smile, Claude says his favourite thing is coffee because it unites society:

'Kings, dictators, ordinary people would not be without coffee anywhere.'

Pushy, capable Jeanne loves her electric guitar and its 'warm wood smell'. Another woman announces, 'I love to cook and I love to feed people. My kitchen is like my office. If you're hungry, come to me, I'll save you.' Banyina, dancing in her seat, says, 'I love music, so my favourite thing is my dancing shoes. Red. Pop them inside.' She mimes grabbing her shoes and throwing them into her bag. 'You can dance anywhere. They make me feel like dancing. They are never uncomfortable.'

Amid all this talk, Manny the musician has been galvanized into action and is actually writing something. And here it is, his favourite thing:

I am wright about my glasses. I have 2 different kind of that. One for reading, another for far. Anfortunetly always I have problem with far glasses. All the time I use it and sometime find damage and I have to go to my local opptition to repair that.

Below it is some writing in Farsi, which I ask him to translate out loud. It's an 'In Memoriam' to his old school music teacher, who had diabetes:

I was in Tehran, the capital city in Iran, at university. I heard he'd died in hospital, during surgery. I was so sad—I'll never forgot how he helped me.

Manny is on a roll and stands up and comes over to me at some point late in the session. He wants to tell me about a bad memory he has. He looks aggrieved, sorting out each word in English, with huge nods of encouragement from me. This is the story, slightly untangled, delivered with a pained, regretful face and almost-tears of shame:

It was a long time ago—I was so young. I was in the street, thinking about a lady I saw, who was a stranger. One time I saw her going in and out of all the houses. I was stupid! In Iran, the women wear headscarves. Suddenly I reached out and pulled off her scarf and saw that under it she was holding a dead chicken that she took from the rubbish, for food, hiding it under the scarf. When I saw that I was crying with shame. So sad. So shame. I was so stupid.

And his happiest memory?

My brother called me and told me, 'I am a father, I had a child, you are an uncle.'

The class finishes in a light mood, mainly because I've ceded any human desire to assist, instruct or improve the group and am simply letting their bossy exuberance wash over me, occasionally rousing myself to shout everyone down so I can hear one reader. There's a core group of about 15, with silent additions on some weeks. The whiteboard, the class plans, the photocopies, the careful prepping, the exercises and my plastic bag of board pens are all forgotten. It's the top of the year and deep winter is thawing slowly. Manny frisks up and whispers to me as he leaves, 'Thank you. A very excited lesson.'

CHAPTER THREE

DEAR DAUGHTER

> Dear Theresa May, Home Secretary,
>
> Can you please give me leave to remain in the United Kingdom? I am not a thief. I am not a terrorist. I am not a drug dealer. I am not a killer, but a peace-loving woman. Thank you.

With this, Glorianna Paston, the grinning woman who made us laugh with her ode to the fat-melting African sun, has produced the most acclaimed piece of writing so far. The class is hooting, crying out in recognition, slapping the tables and urging me to print up the letter, pass it round for everyone to sign and deliver it to the Home Office by hand that very day. Glorianna's chuckling wheezily, hands clasped, her strong face shining all over, ash-grey eyes gleaming. She follows it up with another cheeky note:

> Dear Betty,
>
> I am hereby writing you this letter to apologise for the way I behaved to you the other day in church. I didn't know that the pastor was around. Your loving sister.

Again, as ever, behind the jocularity is a different story. Glorianna is 47 and comes from Sierra Leone. Of her brothers, 'one died in the war in my country, one died last year in June and one remaining. I don't know his whereabouts.' She also has three sisters: 'Two in Africa who ran away from the war in Sierra Leone to Liberia. I haven't heard from them for a long time, but people say they are alive in Liberia. And one sister here who invited me to the UK but I don't know her whereabouts because of one reason or another.' Glorianna has been here for five and half years already and speaks Mende, Krio and English. Her favourite people, she tells me, are her children.

Today we're working on various things, including letters. I give some basic advice on writing official letters, personal messages, academic and job applications and so forth. We do some simple exercises for style and eloquence, like writing a note of gratitude. Most of the students write to friends, contacts at charities, Good Samaritans and near-strangers who have helped them in this country by donating money, assisting with housing and orientation, showing them the ropes and accompanying them on visits.

I'm being beckoned to by the three shady guys in the corner: crutches guy; the streety London-accented Malawian guy with a wolfy smile, whose name is Kafele Chirwa; and a guy with a wide, hard face, acne pocks and short sprouty dreadlocks, whose name is Tejan. Tejan comes from Sierra Leone, has a glinting glance and gives me the almighty instinctive creeps. I'm convinced that he's a militia guy or a drug dealer or a rapist or a killer. It's the way he and his friends get all happy and excited whenever we talk about war and violence, and their evasiveness when it comes to talking about their homes and families, plus a hard flash when they look at me out of the corner of their eyes. My feelings are inflamed all the more when Tejan says with a sigh, 'I miss the BMW I used to drive back in my own country. Now I don't have that. When I see guys driving cars like I used to have . . .' He shakes his head and grizzles in envy and admiration.

But he turns out to be a great raconteur with expert timing. When we're talking about letters we've received that changed our lives, he thinks of a brilliant one that changed a life . . . for the worse:

I knew a guy—a friend of mine from my country. He was in a detention centre. But he couldn't tell his folks back home the truth because it was so awful, so he told them instead, 'Oh, I am living in a five-star hotel! Yes I am. A five-star hotel with three hot meals a day, mmm.' And they thought, 'Oh, Solomon is doing so well!' He told them, 'I have my own sol-ic-it-or. I have my own gen-er-al pract-ition-er.' Because these things are difficult to get in our own country. 'Any day now I will get full unconditional leave to stay. I am a big man.' They thought, 'Oh, Solomon, he's doing so well! Solomon, can you send fifty pounds to fix our car? Fifty pounds is nothing to you. Can you send the money? When can you send the money?' Solomon said, 'Oh yes, no problem, no problem, I will send you the money.' So every week they try to call him: 'Solomon, where is the money to fix the car? Where is that fifty pounds?' 'It's coming, it's coming.' And the weeks pass and they don't hear from him and they call me: 'He said he'd send the money on Thursday but we haven't heard from him, nothing. Where is he?' I said, 'OK, OK, I will find him.' I go to look for him at the place where he's staying. 'Solomon? Solomon? Where are you?' I go down. 'Solomon? Where is Solomon?' I find him. He is in the corner. Down there. He is hiding. 'Solomon, what are you doing? Get up Solomon, your family is asking for you.' He hides his face. On the table is a letter: 'We REFUSE your application for indefinite leave in the UK'! The word REFUSE is so big you don't need glasses to see it! 'You have THE RIGHT to pack up your bags and leave this premises in 24 hours.' The right! *That* is his right.

The class is in an uproar of laughter at the fine telling and the familiar crashdown after such big talk. We break for tea. The group has split between those who rush for the tea and cakes and those who hold back and turn up their noses at such keenness. Same goes for those who do and don't ambush Hannah, the English PEN volunteer who's got travel expenses and reimbursements to hand out. Everybody, it seems, spent exactly eight pounds to get here.

During the break I read something that Beatrice has written:

The best conversation that surely changed my life was one between my father and myself. I was 13 years old, I had sat for my primary school-leaving examinations and had been waiting for the results. One day I was at home in the early afternoon when my father came back home from town. He was walking very fast, panting and excited, and as I wondered why he had come home so early and why he was in such a state, he told me that I had passed my exams, top of my district! This changed my life because I was taken into the best girls' school in my country.

I want to know more about this self-contained woman but my concentration's broken by Mr Loverman, Claude, who's still trying to get a new wife. He offers a Danish pastry to one of the female students, an attractively shrewd type who rejects him. He makes her accept half a Danish and then, as she's about to take a bite, he says, 'I put juju in it.'

She puts it away from her fastidiously.

'No—I don't want no juju. No voodoo,' she says.

'I put juju in it,' he says, satisfied, 'and now you're going to follow me home. Ahh . . .' he leans back and crosses his arms behind his head, 'here I am, surrounded by women.'

Later I learn that he too has been in detention:

'And while I was in there I met lots of Libyans. Libyan refugees. They were in there because nobody believed them either.'

This fits in with what academics Edie Friedman and Reva Klein write in their book *Reluctant Refuge: The Story of Asylum in Britain*, which I've been reading to help give my students' experiences some context:

While in the past anti-asylum sentiment and rhetoric were crude expressions of prejudice, whether in terms of religion, race, economic status or a combination of those factors, more often they have focused on disbelief in claims of persecution. This has not come out of the blue: the government's response to the numbers of people entering this country illegally, itself often a response to media reports, has been negative and punitive.[2]

Meanwhile, Manny wants me to know that his full name is Manuchehr, 'The face of paradise. As you can see right here—the very face of paradise.'

'I am a bit disappointed.'

'I know. Everyone says that. "*This* is the face of paradise?" I am 51. Maybe when I was younger . . .'

I usher everyone back to their desks and prompt a laugh when I say, 'Last time, none of my pens came back to me. The number of pens reduces by 20 per cent every week. And whoever gets my favourite silver pencil, I want it back.'

Manny hands my pens out for me.

'Fifty pence, please,' he jokes to his classmates.

As we try to get started on some work, the women in the class are ragging Don/Dimbi, who won't tell them his real age.

'I have heard four different ages from you,' says one. 'It changes every time.'

2 Edie Friedman and Reva Klein, *Reluctant Refuge: The Story of Asylum in Britain* (London: British Library, 2008), p. 7.

Don tells me he's in his late 60s but he looks much younger, round and solid with his gruff, squinting look. He balls up his fists and flexes his arms.

'We Africans, you see, at 60, we are strong.'

Don's ashamed of his language skills and still hasn't written anything down. When I propose any exercise, he tells me to write it on the board. When break's properly over—including a 10-minute lag to account for what I jokingly call 'international time'—I go straight into an exercise and he looks shocked and says, 'You want us to work now? Just like that?'

'Just like that. It's been 11 minutes already, I'm not here to joke about.'

He wants to tell me his answers out loud.

'Please, write it down,' I say. 'I know you can speak English. Give it to me written and I'll mark it.'

He slumps down and I don't see a word from him all winter. Elodie, who relishes 'exciting thinks', says she'd like to write to her parents thanking them 'for bringing me alive and for educating me and telling me to always be with people who are going to go far'. Jeanne has already filled several sides of paper with sturdy, serviceable prose. She tells me, 'The reason I speak good English is that my parents were exiled and allowed to return, exiled and returned . . .'

Manny says he'd like to write a complaint to the factory who employed him as a casual worker: 'I worked in a sandwich factory in the freezer—big freezer room—and they had eight fans all on my head. And I got a cold. I didn't go for two days and my girlfriend said to me, "What is a cold? Go back." So I went back on the Sunday, and I saw everyone was wearing a hat—a cap?—a cap, and jumper and scarf.'

Don chips in and tells me that he worked in the same factory as Manny, 'One indoors and the other outdoors.'

'You go,' Manny holds out his hand daintily, 'put the things in the tubs, put-put-put-put, in the freezer. So I complained to them, "It is cold!" And they fire me. Russian girls working there now instead.'

I attempt to push my students towards writing a love letter and Manny doesn't want to. He flutters his eyelids and sighs, 'A-a-a-a-artists. We are a-a-a-artists. Always about love and romance.' He mimes writing a letter and begins to sing loudly, 'Ooh-ooh, you are beautiful-l-l-l-l . . .'

'What are you doing?' I ask.

'You told me to write a love letter. This is what you write in a love letter.'

'Bigamy,' says Mr Loverman to me. 'Bigamy is good. Where you're from, there's bigamy.'

'No. There is no bigamy in West Bengal,' I say stiffly.

'I've travelled in West Bengal, there's bigamy everywhere,' he says, looking at me with his cold, heavy, oval eyes, 'in every country in the world.'

A woman rebukes him sharply, putting her nose in the air and saying, 'You have not done a survey of all the regions in all countries and so you cannot say there is bigamy everywhere.'

The complaints and thank-you letters flood out, starting on a funny note by Elodie:

> Dear Stranger, I am writing to complain to you because you are 65 and you are going out with a girl who is 17. I am going to call the police. You are a paedophile. Yours sincerely.

Jeanne writes:

> Dear Dad, I would like to share my sincere apology for not being present at Mum's funeral. The reason being that where I live now in the UK, as an asylum seeker, I am not to leave the country before I am granted a status called Indefinite Leave to Stay.

Banyina and several others write aggrieved letters to landlords and local council people to complain about broken boilers in the hard winters we've been having. A usually meek woman writes, 'I can't really understand how a human being can treat somebody like that. You know very well that we are in winter! And you know my condition. How can you let me stay in a cold house for four days? You promised to come to repair, until now nobody has turn up. I am very very angry.'

Beatrice writes a letter beginning, 'Dear Robinah. I write to thank you for the friendship we share.' When I look it over later I see that the next line—'Since my papers to the Home Office haven't been sorted . . .'—is crossed out. She continues:

> You have been my anchor for a long time, as I have been trying to regularise my stay in the UK. You

have accommodated, fed and given me transport
money. You have enabled me to stay in this country
while I am trying to get indefinite leave to remain.
I thank you most heartedly.

As we finish for the day and pack up, I'm approached
by a silent, smiling woman who sat next to me for the whole
class nodding charmingly. She taps me on the shoulder and
whispers, 'Excuse me. I want to learn how to read and write.
Can you help me?'

I am incredibly embarrassed and point her in the right
direction. When she's gone I look despairingly around the
classroom—unheated, no pens for the whiteboard, crumbs
on the chairs and tables and marks on the floor. Every year
the centre looks after thousands of 'refugees, asylum seekers,
stateless people, victims of human trafficking, separated
families and unaccompanied young people', as it says in its
most recent annual review, adding that many of these people 'have limited or no entitlement to state support or the
right to work. Many live in temporary or insecure accommodation and are victims of crime.' The place is extremely
dynamic, its staff both highly skilled and ferociously committed, and it has a wonderful atmosphere which makes my
heart lift every time I visit. Surely it deserves more help and
better resources?

That day, I kill time in town and then go south on the
Tube. I've begun working with another migrants' resource
centre in Victoria, giving classes in the evenings down in the
basement, which is a kids' nursery during the day. It's fun
working jammed onto buckety plastic chairs in the middle

of piles of toys, games and boxes of jumbo puzzles. We all fall in love with a set of rubber egg timers filled with coloured sand. They're as big as dumb-bells. There's a red one with red sand for 10 minutes, a blue one with blue sand one for 5 minutes and so on. We use them when we're timing the exercises.

The Victoria centre attendees are slightly different from the Bethnal Green ones. They're migrants, but the vast majority are not refugees, asylum seekers or undocumented people. They have leave to stay and work, have more money, privilege, education, support and near-perfect language skills and are generally on their feet and surviving. There's a young, trendy guy from Japan who ran away from home after leaving his parents a 16-page letter telling them he was gay, came to London and married his boyfriend and now wants kids. He tells me he's got a gay Scottish friend who gave his sperm to two lesbian friends and they're all bringing the kid up together very happily. There are two beautiful and clever sisters from Iran, one of whom is a classical dancer and the other a computer engineer looking for a job (I ask my mum, who's a computer scientist, to enquire about hourly teaching at her university), a macho-seeming yet actually monosyllabically shy Syrian guy and several charming Italians with beautiful names: Pierangelo, Emanuele, Ezio and Enrico. There's also a reticent and wry twinkly-eyed Latin American man in his 60s, a Hungarian woman named Tünde who works in the library at a London university, a Sudanese man called Yosof who fled Darfur, first sought asylum in Holland and knows Arabic, Dutch and English and a woman named Marie

Lavoile, in her late 50s or early 60s, who is a francophone African with a mild manner and a very pretty accent.

Marie tells me how hard she has worked to establish herself in England, especially after taking time to bring up her children: 'I have done every course, every workshop, every guidance meeting, every qualification. I have been for every interview. But you realize there is an age when they don't want you, and that is very depressing.'

The man next to her suddenly grabs her tightly, squeezes her, shakes her—she is so startled and unconsenting that she stares down into her lap in shock—and squeals loudly in grating patronage, 'No-o-o-o! *I* want you!'

She shakes off the unwanted contact and doesn't look at him.

The students in this second group greet me smoothly and work diligently on all the tasks I set them. When they've done the exercises they read them out, listening to each other respectfully. If I give them feedback they take it in. Then they wait for me to tell them the next exercise to do. I look at their intelligent and attractive faces, hear their polished words, observe their good manners and sorely miss being pushed around by my morning group, who leave me so intrigued and exhausted that I can barely crawl to the Museum of Childhood afterwards to eat a comforting children's-food lunch bowl of macaroni cheese.

There are some interesting stories in the second group, however. This is Marie's 'Letter to Maman'. It's headed, 'London, England, February 2012' and continues:

Dearest Maman,

I am writing to let you know that you are constantly on my mind. You said I have become a different person and I don't care as much as I used to. Maman, I really care more than you could ever imagine. I know that I have not been able to do as much as you wanted me to do. However, I have been doing exactly what you did when you were bringing up your family. Every two years I had a little brother or sister who needed your attention. You did what was best for your children and you put them first before anything or anybody else.

For example, you gave up your teaching career for them. I remember also those nights when I or my siblings were sick, you took the portable lamp and went to the neighbour to buy what was needed to make us feel better. I appreciated those loving acts then, and now as a mother I do appreciate them even more. Maman, you are my role model.

Further, the weekends you have spent making me pretty dresses to go to Mass on Sundays are not forgotten. I want you to know that I do the same for my children. Maman, did you know that you started a trend long before it became popular around the world? Yes, I remember how you used to cut your long black hair to use as extensions for my short hair. Unfortunately, I can't do the same for my daughter because her hair is longer than mine.

Please Maman dear, don't judge me by the pretty dresses and the smile that I am wearing in the photographs that I have sent home. They are camouflage to disguise the real reasons why I stay away for so long. Life did not deliver what it had promised me. However, what it gave me I have used to the best of my ability.

Maman, you ask me repeatedly if I am going to let you die without seeing you. I really, truly, desperately want to see you. I know it has been almost 38 years since I last saw you, and you are now 85 years old. Please Maman, don't die, I am longing to see you. Please wait for me! I am counting on divine assistance to make this year the year that I see you again.

Your loving daughter,

Bibine

I am exhausted by the first few lots of doing two several-hour blocks of teaching in one day, organizing my notes from each session and transcribing what I've memorized. So it's a while before I spot two letters that were written in the Bethnal Green morning class but not read out. The first is from Beatrice. It's unfinished. It starts:

Dear Joseph, I am writing this letter to you but it's not for you alone. It's for all of my children. This letter is an explanation of why I made the decision to leave you behind in Uganda and come to the UK. It was a hard decision to make but you were still young and I could never have explained to you then.

The second letter is by Glorianna Paston, who made us laugh with her ode to the African sun and her letter to Theresa May. It goes like this:

Dear daughter, I am writing this letter to tell you exactly what happened between me and your dad. It was during the war in our country, and by then you were a toddler so you can't remember anything. I was raped by the rebels and was trying to hide it from your dad. I don't know how he came to know about it, but since then he don't want me any more in his life. My dear daughter, can you please talk to your dad so that he take me back home?

CHAPTER FOUR

HER LOVELY EYES

Manny comes in early and sits down while I organize myself. He watches me benignly, tall and bright-faced, with that beautiful Iranian mountain colour, dusky yet icy.

'Sorry. I'm just arranging things,' I say.

'No, no, not at all. Thank you for talking to me.'

I giggle. He giggles. On the pitted grey walls of the classroom are tolerance posters: *You have a right not to be attacked for your sexuality, race, sex, country, religion, colour* . . . There are also leaflets for conversational English classes at entry level, guides to gaining legal representation and accessing family health care.

'You're very highly educated,' I say. 'Why can't you work here?'

'You can't if it's in the arts. If I were a doctor, yes. I have some students of Iranian music here. But not a proper job. In France, where I was before, they had some beautiful Iranian music classes. In my country, I was a teacher in a university when I was 30 years old. Young. And me and my students, we were always laughing, laughing, laughing. Sometimes, they laughed at me. Sometimes,' he drolly concedes, 'they were absent. . . . In Iran,' he says after a while, 'in my country, they don't have any foreigners. They are very strict. But here, there are so many languages, so many cultures, different colours, different people.'

'That's the case in London and in the major cities. It may not be the case further out.'

'Aha. They'll have that thing.'

'What thing?'

'What's that thing, where the white doesn't like the black, the black doesn't like the white . . .'

'Oh—do you mean racism?'

'Yes!'

I'm still arranging when everyone else comes in talking, joking and rebuking one another at the tops of their voices. The regular students sit down and look at me patiently, ignoring the ones who've decided to visit out of curiosity. To the regulars, my name in the first few weeks was either Beddish or Anisha. After a while, they dumped all that and just call me Teacher. I don't mind.

Every week, there are new faces. They say nothing, just look at me with silent challenge or silent dolefulness or silent query or a tinge of embarrassment or a shade of misery. And there have begun to be small children in the class, too. I smile at the kids, call them things like 'little tiger' and find pens and paper for them. None of the new adult faces pretends to do any work. They sit in the farthest corners and at the edges, watching, waiting, heavy and guarded.

Mr Loverman is standing about, clucking and strutting like a big pigeon. His volubility has turned into a rather hard, insistent sleaziness that not a single woman in the class is charmed by. He makes tea for the women sitting near him, particularly the older women.

'I am the only gentleman left,' he sighs. He says to refined, fragile Rose, who was gifted a gold watch by her grandchildren, 'Auntie, are you all right? I am always happy to see you.'

She trembles and is mutely circumspect. Claude says to his friends in French, 'I have a girlfriend but not a wife.'

'Why can't you turn your girlfriend into a wife?' I ask.

'I can't jump the step. Every time, there is a step. I cannot cross to the next stage. Before you buy the sugar, you try it in the tea.'

He has met his match, however, in Glorianna Paston, who sits big and tough in her seat, watching him with her shining, solid face and lightless grey-black eyes. She snaps her fingers at him when he's still going on 10 minutes later, 'How many wives do you want? Two? I'll find you two good ones. Two. No problem.'

Having had his bluster deflated, Mr Loverman is appalled and doesn't know where to look, saying feebly, 'I don't need help! I can find two wives. I have eyes.'

'Yes, but sometimes you need a little help with introductions,' I say.

The class is restless today and when I make a chance comment—something about 'why we're all here'—they all explode.

'We cannot go back, they will rape us and kill us. Our countries' leaders don't care about us, only about the oil, the minerals, everything they can take out of the earth,' says Jeanne starkly.

Crutches guy—who still hasn't told me his name and hasn't written anything—gets fired up. 'We didn't want to leave our countries! Because of wars we became refugees. Because of imperialism there were wars in countries that weren't at war before, until the English arrived. This is capitalist imperialism. The British—the English—went anywhere they wanted but no one called them illegal immigrants or asylum seekers or threw them in detention centres. They could create slaves and wars and poverty in any land they wanted. They took what they wanted. None of this was here before. My father's father was a trader across Africa, he would be away for weeks and he said he remembers trading across three countries—there were no borders. Then suddenly there were borders, mines, police, guns, wars. War is the most profitable thing. You sell weapons, sell arms, sell minerals, you trade, you set up dictators to punish each other. Then you have refugees, asylum seekers, running away from wars.'

I'm intrigued by this man. He tells me nothing about his current life, his family or his history, except what is revealed by accident. Yet despite his anger and his clearly hand-to-mouth existence, the heart of what he says about Africa is backed up by academics Lothar Brock, Hans-Henrik Holm, Georg Sørensen and Michael Stohl in their book *Fragile States*, a study of war and conflict in the modern world. They write:

In many cases [fragile states] are ex-colonies settled within the borders established by the colonial powers. [. . .] The colonial powers took no particular interest in the political and economic development of the areas of which they took possession in Africa. They were more interested in maximising profits, so their focus was on the extraction and export of natural resources, combined with an effort to curtail their cost of controlling the colonies. [. . .] In some places [in Africa] colonial rule involved building some infrastructure, together with some political as well as economic institutions. But any such measure remained focused on the cities, not on the countryside. The colonial jurisdictions in Africa were created and later redrawn, trimmed down or enlarged—without any consultation with, or consideration for, the indigenous peoples.[3]

The various criteria which they cite to indicate fragile statehood fit in with many of my students' experiences. According to the Failed States Index provided by the Fund for Peace and *Foreign Policy*, the indicators include the mass movement of refugees or internally displaced persons; a legacy of vengeance-seeking group grievance, smaller militias and militarized rebels and factions within territories;

---

3 Lothar Brock, Hans-Henrik Holm, Georg Sørensen and Michael Stohl, *Fragile States: War and Conflict in the Modern World* (Cambridge: Polity, 2012), p. 29.

severe economic decline; the criminalization or delegitimization of the state; the progressive deterioration of public services; the suspension or arbitrary application of the rule of law and the widespread violation of human rights.

I had been counselled before these classes not to push my students for their stories. I am to keep things light and current and look to the future, so we go for positivity and draw some 'Mind Maps': visions of our lives, and of the various parts of our lives. There's one version for life as it is now and another for life as we would like it to be.

'What are the basics of a life?' I ask.

'Home,' says everyone.

I put Home at the centre.

'Family. Friends. Money,' suggests the group.

'Religion?' I ask. I put that in its own segment. Many of the African students are Catholic but no one seems particularly exercised on this point.

'Work. Education. Health,' the group adds.

The Work segment is blanket bad news for everyone. They do voluntary work, off-the-books work, grey-market work, unstable work, work which confers no rights. Under this segment of the Mind Maps, we write 'Unemployment—no papers, no accreditation—not allowed to work.' There is a thick sense of gall and frustration, of stifled and wasted life, given the level of education among the group. Most of my students are in their prime and all speak multiple languages. There is not a single person in the room that is not educated to some level after school. Manny has a PhD, many have degrees, many have been to college and all have had jobs. They were not chancers and derelicts in their own countries, or crooks or scroungers. They ask me to explain what NVQs, HSCs and other British vocational qualifications are and I talk them through the various levels of attainment.

Loverman tells me he has a degree in criminology and complains, 'When you go to a new country, even if you are educated, your education is not accepted as being at the same level.'

'Meanwhile,' someone adds, 'when people from here want good medical care they go to India for treatment by the doctors there!'

'Now,' I say, putting my board pen up to a new section of the Mind Map. 'Money.'

Everyone just laughs. We move onto the ideal-but-realistic version of our Mind Maps.

'Living with all your children, or as many of them as you can,' says one woman.

'Being able to take holidays together,' says another.

'Houses,' I prompt.

'Mansions! Buckingham Palace!'

'I am rich. I am rich I tell you,' says Banyina of the red dancing shoes. 'My bank account is full. It's heavy! I am flying to Africa tomorrow in a gold plane.'

Joking aside, the places they want to live are modest: there are multiple bids for Peckham, Brixton and Camden and a breakaway contingent in favour of Kingston and Richmond. Many simply want to continue living in the Greater

London suburbs where they already are but just be able to work and support themselves.

When we talk about work, Tejan the scary guy from Sierra Leone clenches his fists and vigorously says, 'Army. Protecting home and family.'

I gag slightly and can't meet his eye. One of the group members shouts at him, 'Huh! You want to be in the Congolese army?'

Many say they want to be carers, look after children, be community workers or teachers while others say the most solid jobs are to be a barrister or a doctor. Jeanne would like to teach music, sewing and singing in her local community and I have no doubt, with her toughness, that she will achieve this. A large minority of the class want to attain self-sufficient stability so that they can help other asylum seekers trying to find their feet.

But the challenges of employment are nothing compared to the caprices of the English language.

'Cough, rough, Gough, Hough, through, plough, enough,' I say during the next section of the lesson, as the class tries to sound out the different words without any help from me. 'They're pronounced differently but spelt the same. I don't know why. There's no rule. You're just going to have to memorize them. Now: sea bass, the fish. Bass, the register in music. And base, the bottom of something. A length of string can get all snarled up,' I show them a line from an Elisabeth Bishop poem about a knotted kite string, 'or I can snarl at you like *this*.'

I snarl.

'Snarling is what lions do,' says someone.

During a dip in the proceedings, I'm approached by lovely, sloppy Elodie. She tells me she's applying for a job as a tour guide at the Wallace Collection.

'Aha! Good idea! I am very glad you're doing that,' I say, though I secretly doubt her English skills are up to it.

'I love Elodie because she has gone from completely French to completely English,' says one of the other young women in the group, who's standing next to Elodie supportively.

Hmm. Elodie writes with great wit and confidence in fully phonetic Franglais. Her English seems good when I hear it, but when I read it it's all 'pliz' for please and 'consil' for council.

'Let's have a look,' I say.

The advert says that Elodie must make a five-minute presentation about art, culture, the Wallace Collection itself, her education and her experience as a tour guide.

'Give me one line to say under all the headings,' she tells me.

I try my best. Whatever I say, off the top of my head, she writes down verbatim.

'Elodie, have you ever been to the Wallace Collection?'

'Yeah,' she says breezily in her deep-voiced Frenchy Cockney. Then, 'No.'

'Have you ever been to a museum in London?'

'I have been to the . . . Bar-bi-can?'

'The Barbican! In East London! OK! That's good!'

'I can say I like to go to film. Eddie Murphy film. *Coming to America.*'

'OK . . . that did come out a few years ago . . . like in the 80s.'

'I can say I went skiing at Hackney Empire. Is that culture?'

I think she means ice skating. Unless the Hackney Empire put up a fake ski slope one Easter.

'I'm not sure that quite counts . . .'

'I don't know art. I know Picasso only.'

I urge her to go onto the Wallace Collection website, look through it, see what draws her eye and learn the names and histories of some of the pieces she likes. Then I cross my fingers and tell her to let me know how it all went.

At the end of the class, Beatrice comes up to me. She has several pieces of lined A4 paper written through in her crisp, adult hand and kept carefully in thin plastic sleeves.

'I'd like to finish the letter to my son,' she says. 'Not just a short letter but a long letter, telling him everything in stages, from the beginning. How I came to this country, why I had to leave Uganda and all the things that have happened. And all the things I've been through. But it is a long thing.'

'I'll help you,' I say, basking in her smooth warm glow. 'But I don't think you need my help. I think you just need to do it. Plan it and do it. But it'll be two years' work.'

She nods serenely and shows me the plan she's already done:

My first 13 years: birth to primary 7.

My secondary school years: senior 1 to 6.

My college years; marriage; birthing children; working life.

Working life continued: accounting, business, teaching, then moving to the UK.

The UK: London, Crawley in Sussex, London [again], Lydd in Kent, Perranporth in Cornwall, Portishead in Bristol, Weston Super Mare, Whitley in Surrey, Chorley Wood in Herts, Ilford, Redbridge, Bethnal Green, Leatherhead in Surrey.

I stare in shock at the long list of places she's been moved around to.

'I thought, if I do it in stages, and I give them to you to look at . . .' she says.

'Of course, of course.'

She gives me some of the papers.

'Shall I photocopy them?' I ask.

'I made copies.' She has done them, carefully, by hand. 'I want it to be finished, somehow, so that he can read it.'

'Well, I'm making notes about these sessions, just simple notes. If you want to give them to me, I'd be happy to type them up. They might be published—with your name, of course.'

'That would be nice,' she says.

And that is how we begin.

That evening in the nursery, I talk to my second group about the small triumphs of living in a new country. One of the two Persian sisters, both of whom we are all indulgent towards because they're so clever and talented and beautiful and sweet and radiant, says her triumph was making herself go into a library and request a library card in English. There is a Latin American woman who forced herself to become fluent in English and do the one thing she had always dreamt of—completing a PhD in psychology. Yet she hasn't found a position to match her education. Many of this group are looking for work, just like my other lot. Enrico, an architect, says he can only pick up short-term contracts for small projects.

Yosof says his biggest triumph was learning Dutch. He had fled Darfur and arrived in the Netherlands assuming everyone in Europe spoke English. He learnt to speak fluently and then got a full degree in maths from a Dutch university before coming to Britain.

'What a shock. Dutch,' he says ruefully.

I get out our favourite chunky egg timers and my students write about cherished things while I try to memorize what's in the nursery. There's a big poster headed 'We Are Learning About People Who Help Us'. Another section of the wall's dedicated to 'Our Favourite Animals'. Mobiles and artworks hang from the ceiling. Then there are the smiling pictures and perky details of some of the students, whose names reflect the diversity of the area: Shyne, Santiago, Victory, Naz, Arif, Aisha, Asha, Denas, Samson, Sulima.

Yosof has written a piece called 'A Bright Silver Ring':

I wear it sometimes on my right hand's middle finger, yet sometimes I wear it on the left hand's middle finger. It is a bright big silver ring which had been given to me by my older sister. 'It makes no difference where to wear it,' said my sister when I visited her for the last time at her present home in Niyala.

Niyala is one of the biggest cities in the west of Sudan. Her home where she used to live with her seven children, and her husband of course, covers an area of not more than 50 square metres. They lived in that house for several years. They eat, drink and sleep in that small area. They are the happiest family ever I have seen.

She was hugging me while pressing something hard in my right hand, something hard as a ring. I closed my hand around it without showing it to the other people. I kissed her between her lovely eyes when I said farewell to sister Zaynab.

Yosof writes that he remembers his sister every time someone asks about the ring. It's a big, white-shining silver square with writing embossed on the flat facing part.

'What does it say?' I ask.

This grown man with a thin, intelligent face gives a glowing smile, shakes his head and boyishly hides the ring from view under the table.

'It's private,' I smile. 'You don't want to say.'

CHAPTER FIVE

THAT IS NOT WHAT I AM

'Late! Who is late? Teacher is late!'

It's Manny. He's caught me running along the road, my overcoat flapping around my knees. He ushers me in and up the stairs with airy sweeps of his arms. In his high, thin voice he tells me he's been ill, 'A chest infection, I have been in the hospital.'

'You're always ill.'

'Three times now I had this,' he mournfully agrees, before showing me into the waiting room and announcing to everyone, 'Teacher is late!'

'Don't look at me,' I say to them, hiding my face.

'I discovered her on the street,' says Manny. 'She was running.'

We get into our room, sit down and shiver.

'I am sorry but it is completely freezing,' says someone to me.

The little fan heater hunkers on the floor and breathes out weakly. It's cold and grey and rain-streaked outside. Today, we're doing poetry.

'There is no such thing as a bad poem,' I lie.

We talk about style and rhyme, about avoiding repetition and what makes a poem a poem.

'A feeling. A mood. Atmosphere,' say my students.

'Ah, but you also need discipline, form and shape,' I say.

'Facts,' says someone.

'But you can also write a poem that's fiction. And a poem has to go somewhere. It needs an arc. Not necessarily a story.'

'No sad stories,' says someone firmly.

We agree to write five lines based on something that's in the room, everything from the fluorescent lights to the furniture, the carpet (blue scrub, smeared with dirt), cables (covered in sticky dust), whiteboard (covered in my comments from the previous week, half rubbed out) to the posters on the wall. *Are you worried about someone you know?* asks a poster next to a large, torn world map.

'And we can write about you,' says Manny.

'No, you will not.'

'You are in the room.'

Next to the whiteboard is a big paper scribble pad on an easel. There are language and orientation classes here on other days. On the pad is written, 'HE gives HER a present. SHE gives HIM a present.' With a drawing of a stick man and a stick woman.

I am challenged by Don, who still has not written a word for me to see, to make up a poem or give him an idea on the spot.

'All right then . . . I found someone's front-door key on the street the other day, in Euston,' I say, 'and it made me think about all the lost items and lost people in the city. And I was thinking that with the key I'd be able to unlock a different city underneath London, a reversed city where things are all the opposite from here, and that in it would be all the lost things that need keys, like travel locks and suitcases, safes, front doors, houses, lockets, diaries. Secret vaults. And then I thought, what'd happen if only special people could see the keys and the hidden things? And perhaps the keys were deliberately left scattered about London by some secret group, to identify the special people.'

They like this.

'Tips: do not describe what a key looks like literally or what it does. We all know that. Describe what it makes you think about, what its meaning might be to you, how it makes you feel or what it makes you hope for or remember,' I say.

Elodie impresses us by reading out the following:

I am drunk and I'm walking home, being followed
by two strangers. I'm so scared. I can't find my door
key. Key, this is not the time to play. Can't you tell
there are strangers behind me? Stop hiding.

But when I look at the longer, written version later, my heart sinks:

I dronk a lot and I'm working there two people who
are follow me am so scar where are you. I am near
the house where are you don't you think it's not the
time to play don't you think those people are
stronger [strangers] to me. Oh! Now I find you.

Banyina writes an impassioned ode to her table, which she delivers with wailing emotion:

Oh ta-a-a-a-ble. Ta-a-a-ble! Grey. Smooth. With your four strong legs you hold things up. What would I do without you ta-a-a-a-ble?

No one is taking this seriously at all. I propose something in two parts, one paragraph about how my students think people see them and another about how they really are. Claude drops his Loverman persona to display some of his natural, suspicious intelligence: 'It is very difficult because no one will be critical of themselves. I am a secretive man. I don't like to open up the book of my life to other people.'

Yet the other day, when he was patrolling the classroom and talking up the ladies he said to them, 'I am a talkative man.'

'Come on Claude, I know you have a degree in criminology,' I say lightly.

Immediately his face closes up, his eyes go cold and he stares at me in mistrust.

'How do you know?' he asks in an icy voice, so different from his usual manner.

'You told me.'

He looks caught out and incredibly cheesed off with himself for having revealed a small true detail in between all his banter. I suggest that we get started by everyone writing one particular thing about themselves, all on the same piece of paper, which we'll pass around the class. They refuse. They each want to write down the thing privately and hand it to me.

'Why?' says Kafele, the lively Malawian guy with the London accent and the fierce grin, to the rest of the class. 'It's not like anyone's told you to get naked.'

'Are poetry and poems the same?' asks Don.

'Aha! Now I'm teaching,' I say. I write on the board, 'Poetry produces poems. Poems are made of poetry. You are a poet. A poet uses poetry to write a poem.'

That should clear things up. Kafele has a bit of writing for me and it's good too:

In the evening, from the sea, we can see how the
jungle was shaped. It looked like a lion's mountain.
The wind was so strong that our sea vessel ended
up smashed into pieces.

His friend in the shady corner next to him—crutches guy, still rickety and rackety, still nameless, although I notice he doesn't actually have his crutches with him today—has one of his periodic outbursts of eagerness: 'I'm not going to write it down, I'll tell you. I'm a roofer, yeah, in Blackfriars. I was walking along the street afterwards, smoking. It was a green man, time to cross, a van came out of nowhere and hit me. I fell over. I looked. It was a white van. I looked, I saw the driver. He was laughing. Laughing at me. I couldn't believe it. He was laughing. I lost my kneecap.'

'So *that's* why you've been on crutches . . .'

'Yeah! I have no kneecap. I was in hospital for nine months—I have metal, metal in my leg—not a bar. A plate. I thought I was finished but—but—God is great! My doctor, he was Indian. He told me, 'You will walk. You will run!'

The driver, the police found him, he was drunk. They suspended his licence. He didn't even bother to come to court. And the other day . . . I was almost run down again.'

I take all this in and return, dazed, to face the whiteboard, but he calls me back again: 'I was working on a building site, that's what I do now, I'm a crane operator, and all day I was with this guy, he didn't want to do it. He was afraid.'

'He was afraid of heights?'

'Yeah! Anyway, at the end of the day we came down for our money and the boss of the building site, I'm sorry to say, he was an Asian.'

'That's all right.'

'Yeah, he gave me money and there was a lot. A lot of money. And the guy who was with me all day, he had only a little, and he said, "Why does he get a lot of money and I get a little?" And the man said, "Oh, you didn't work, you didn't do anything." And the guy was really upset.'

'Does that happen a lot? People being underpaid for building work?'

'All the time. All the time.'

'Because the money's paid unofficially, and a lot of the workers are undocumented?'

'Yes. So they treat you how they want.'

'Do they sometimes not pay at all?'

'Oh yes! Oh yes.'

'They say, "Come back tomorrow, you'll get paid then, or you're fired," ' say other people in the class.

David J. Whittaker, writing in his book *Asylum Seekers and Refugees in the Contemporary World*, backs up what I'm learning. He describes the casual employment of refugees and asylum seekers as 'a nefarious form of integration'. He adds:

> Over perhaps decades, a network has sprung up of bogus 'advisors', fraudulent landlords and plainly dishonest agents and entrepreneurs, touting job opportunities. They know all the loopholes [. . .] there are no questions asked in 'Job Street'. Nor are there work permits, nor ready money agreements, nor rights. An underclass is pinned down by a 'black economy' where the gang master rules. [. . .] They [illegal workers] are the 'invisibles' [. . .] all too often ignored by the rest of society.[4]

'And I have another story,' says crutches guy, 'I won't write it, I'll tell you. I was sleeping on a bench next to a church, behind, you know, St Paul's?'

'Yes?'

'I was sleeping on the bench. I was drunk,' he says emphatically.

Everyone's listening, smiling naughtily. I'm not quite sure if this is what one of my prepping papers, a sincere, long and well-meaning essay published as *The Art of Helping Others: Being Around, Being There, Being Wise* by Heather Smith

---

4 David J. Whittaker, *Asylum Seekers and Refugees in the Contemporary World* (London: Routledge, 2006), p. 33.

and Mark K. Smith, quite meant when it recommended that teachers should be 'building communities of truth' and 'nurturing moments of reflection and connection.'[5]

'And I needed to shit,' says crutches guy. 'So I found a plastic bag and I opened it and I . . .' He gets up, crouches a little and mimes unbuckling his belt, shoving his trousers down over his stuck-out arse and doing a shit. 'So I begin to shit.'

'Hang on. Were you homeless?'

'Yeah! So I was doing the shit and suddenly I heard next to me, in the shadows, there was a person. It was a policeman. You know the Met? Metropolitan Police? It was a policeman. But I couldn't stop. I couldn't stop the shit, so I shit. And he begins to piss. The policeman, he begins to piss by the, you know, the wall.'

'You're taking a drunken shit in the shadows of a famous cathedral, behind the bench you've been sleeping on, while an unseen policeman takes a piss?'

'Be strong, Teacher, be strong,' cries Don supportively.

'So I finish the shit and I tie up the bag and . . .' Crutches guy mimes putting the tied bag away from him, pulling up his trousers, re-buckling his belt and straightening his coat. 'And then the policeman hears me. He says, "Who's there?" I come out. He says, "Who are you?" He cuffed me. They always cuff me. He asks me what am I doing here? I say, "I'm doing a shit."'

5 Heather Smith and Mark K. Smith, *The Art of Helping Others: Being Around, Being There, Being Wise* (London: Jessica Kingsley, 2008), p. 93.

'Did he arrest you for anything?'

'No. And then, he was smoking. You know. Smoking weed.'

'No!'

'Yes!'

'Outrageous.'

'Yes! A policeman. He was smoking weed by the wall after taking a piss.'

'Outrageous!'

'*Yes.*'

I back away, consoled by another quote from *The Art of Helping Others*: 'In many respects the act of listening to a person's story and showing that we have heard what they have said is one of the most helpful things we can do.'[6]

In the end, crutches guy and the policeman did a deal, promising not to tell on each other. A colleague from English PEN drops in at about this time, thinks that we're discussing literature, looks around approvingly and calls out, 'Wonderful! Wonderful!'

'We don't get much work done but you can't say we're not having a good time,' I say, weakly.

In a burst of confidence, I ask if anyone would be interested in doing art workshops and creative writing. Two people put up their hands.

'OK,' I say. 'Maybe not.'

6 Ibid., p. 99.

Banyina tells me that it was the same with the music workshops. The interest only grew when the posters went up: 'If you ask people, they'll say they don't want to.'

Jeanne, striking in a sharp red beret, black jumper and fat white pearls, goes straight up to my PEN colleague and says, 'Are there different levels of workshops I can attend? Is there a level higher than this?'

The colleague is polite and taken aback and says apologetically that, no, there is not. Poor Jeanne, cursed with a mixture of traits that would be awkward in any culture: clever, sensitive yet insensitive, aggressive yet community-minded, tough, pushy, arrogant yet gifted, striving. She keeps loading me up with her work and then complaining that the previous booklet produced by PEN gave multiple pages to other people who had submitted their writing but relatively little space to her. Then she cringes, beams at me with a hard eye and says in a high, wavering warble, 'Oh, I am so nervous about my writing. I'm not sure if I am doing it right or not.'

'I'm sure it's fine,' I say, but can't help a flicker of irritation every time we finish an exercise and her hand is the first to go up, followed by the immediate reading out of her work, in a dry, low, prating voice, while the others fidget. She has no close friends in the group and often tells them off for talking too loudly or laughing too much. By now she is actually sitting at the corner of my desk.

In her piece about how strangers see her she says, 'Strangers never know where in Africa I come from. They sometimes think I do not know how to express myself or write English, that is to say, very illiterate, but then get a surprise when I talk or write. Sometimes strangers from Africa talk to me in Ghanaian languages.'

Malawian shady-guy Kafele gives me the chills by writing, 'I think people see me as somebody very friendly, considerate and good-looking to every point but I do see myself as a syndicate executioner. But sometimes I feel very vulnerable as well.'

Banyina says that when people meet her they think of her as straightforward, funny and friendly, 'and then they ask if I am Jamaican. I say, "No, I am from Cameroon. I'm Cameroonian." They say, "Not Jamaican?"'

We laugh sadly over these misassumptions and talk about how few people know that Africa is not a country but a continent with more than 50 countries in it, including countries in what we think of as the Middle East region.

Jeanne says in her fierce yet abject way, 'When people meet me, they think I am stupid and uneducated, and then I open my mouth and they are shocked. I speak and I point out their mistakes and then they're *really* shocked.'

In the few minutes before break time, some of the students want to complete their 'Mind Maps' from last week. Sitting near Beatrice is another quiet woman, much less confident than Beatrice, with a smaller voice and a neat frame. Her name is Clara Butoye, she's 63 and from Burundi, has been in the UK for 11 years, lives in Hackney and speaks French, Swahili, Lingala and English. I think her spirits are struggling a bit because under Work she writes, 'I can't work because of my back' and under Education, 'I can't continue

to study because of my age.' 'If I was in good health I would
have worked in this country,' she adds. Under Money, 'I
don't have money because I don't work.' And love? 'Love
must be a proper one.'

Beatrice's own mind map is a little less despairing. She
writes that she has 'No money since I don't work. I get lots
of financial help from friends.' But, 'I would like to earn my
own money, pay my own bills.' She lives with a friend in
temporary accommodation and her health is 'Good, a few
headaches when stressed.' Under Education she's written
that she studied in Uganda to 'college and university level'.
She has '5 children, 4 of them over 18. I have my father, 5
brothers and 6 sisters. All in Uganda.' She would like 'To
own my own home in Woodford, East London, to be able
to work, to learn how to use the computer to excellence and
study for a Masters degree in English. I would like to get a
responsible man friend that I can share the rest of my life
with. I would like to be living with some of my children and
with my friends all still around so we can share our lives.'

Tough, funny Glorianna Paston has written in the centre, under Home, 'No home. Displaced.' She is educated to
college level. Money? 'No money, I survive by friends.' She'd
like to be living with her children. Under Family she's written, 'Rejected by families, supported by friends.'

At break time there's the usual rush for expenses, not
from my regular students but from the silent new additions
among whom word has got around that if you sit through
three hours of my teaching, you can get eight pounds. This
is what poverty makes people do. It has become particularly

obvious these past few weeks: last week there were four new silent men; this week there are two new kids including a little unhappy one who cries (Manny plays with him) and an inquisitive toddler who's fascinated by the wheelchair/trolley ramp and the swing doors and keeps having to be called back. The people doing it are not graspers, criminals, freeloaders or malicious thieves trying to swindle a system but silent, embarrassed individuals, looking at me not with triumph but with baleful, bitter dispirit. They're not cheating the centre. The staff here know what's going on and what it's like for them, so some resources are reserved for this kind of thing. Anyway, if I had to sit through one of my lessons, I'd claim much more than eight pounds' compensation.

Still, the behaviour of the new arrivals has angered the regulars in the class. A very bright young woman who's been showing great insight with our poetry exercises looks askance at one of the women jostling my colleague who's trying to keep track of names and expenses.

'She will die there, in that crowd,' tuts my student. 'So desperate to get their money. It's not responsible. I know I will get my money. They should line up one by one, not crowd round like that.'

Beatrice comes up to me and tells me she's been writing a lot during the last week. She's continued her letter to her son, 'because I have to tell him everything, and also some details about my mother and my grandmother, when I remember to put them in. I was thinking, it'll be maybe three books.'

'But your son won't read all three?'

'But he should.'

'Write it all down from beginning to end but be streamlined and disciplined,' I counsel.

She shows me the part of her plan that deals only with her arrival in the UK and the way she was moved around and tried to get her bearings.

'Maybe I should only do the part of me in England, if English people are going to read it?'

'No, no, believe me,' I reassure her, 'readers in this country like to read about all countries and all backgrounds. We want to know where you're from, when you were a child, where you lived and what it was like.'

'But there are things I want to explain and I don't know the word in English, only in my own language.'

'Like what?'

'Like, we had baskets . . .'

'Hmm?'

'And . . . like this . . .' She takes off her woollen scarf, tightens it, then wraps it into a loose coil about the size of a quarter-plate and tucks the ends inside.

'Are you talking about weaving?' I ask.

'No.' She holds the coiled scarf up and bounces its soft–stiff Danish pastry shape in her hand. She explains, 'We have baskets and carry them on our heads, but to make a sort of pad, and to make the baskets balance, we take something, like reeds, and we make them into one of these and put them on our heads before the basket.'

'Aha! I see that! You coil it up to make a pad.'

'But there's no word for it in English. I only know the word in my own language. Can I put it in?'

'Of course you can, and then you can explain it, exactly as you explained it to me.'

As she leaves, she gives me the work she did in class this morning and says, 'You asked how other people see us. In this country, sometimes they see us as primitive, as animals. They think we are uneducated, that we don't know how to use the toilet. Someone said to me,' she holds up her hand and slowly mimes flicking a wall switch, '"This is how you turn on a light." Do they think we don't know how to turn on a light? That we never had a light? I don't say anything, because I don't want to offend them.'

She has written under How People See Me:

People think I never went to school. They think I don't know how to use modern gadgets. They think I don't know how to write. 'Do you know how to write?' they ask me. 'Can you read?' they ask me. 'Did you wash your hands?' after I've been to the toilet. 'Is it always dark in Africa?' Why? 'Because it is called the dark continent.' Helpful they are, showing me how to switch on the kettle to make a cup of tea. Helpful they are, showing me how to turn on the light in my new room.

Primitive? No, that is not what I am. I have been to school. I have read Shakespeare. In another country, in another century. I have done experiments in physics and in chemistry, in a laboratory, on another continent. I know how to add, subtract and multiply. I can solve a mathematical equation. I know how to draw a map. I have sung at the Barbican, in this country, in this century.

Under How I See Myself she has written:

I see myself as I am really, a middle-aged lady living on a continent I wasn't born in, with hope for a better future, never misplaced or misunderstood again.

CHAPTER SIX

THE FOLK SONG THAT NEVER WAS

One of the previous classes in my room clearly had an apocalyptic theme: on the whiteboard are the words Pollution, Biodegradable, Good/Bad Habit, Central Line, Oyster Card, Congestion Charge. When the end of the world comes, exacerbated by pollution and our bad habit of not using biodegradable products, flee on the Central Line, remembering to touch in and out with your Oyster Card. But if you're escaping Armageddon in your car, don't forget to pay the congestion charge.

By 11 a.m., no one is in. I stand there reading the poster from Carers Direct: *If you look after someone, who looks after you?* There's also a list of classes run for a local women's group, offering certificates in childcare and beauty therapy but also providing help for new mums, mothers who want to help kids with their homework, a crèche, keep fit ('First come first served, small charge of £1') and a self-defence class. The room's empty and I hear loud, laughing voices deep inside the building. Another poster: *Worried someone close to you is losing their memory?* Another poster: *Workshop on vulnerable adults and adults at risk.*

It's sunny and almost warm outside today, for the first time since I began here. Is that why they haven't turned up?

I go down the empty corridor, past the music hall and back into reception, where I find all my students sitting in a row on the plastic chairs. They turn their heads and look at me gently, like sunbathers gazing out to sea.

'What! Why are you all waiting here like patients at the GP? Are you mad?'

Softly, slowly, they follow me in. They're in a holiday mood and everyone's wearing bright, beautiful summer clothes. I spot a gentleman in a striking red and white striped shirt printed crisply with black and white footballs, a woman in a gold brocade stole, another in an orange, pink and cream floor-length smock with pink headwrap and green leather slippers. Elodie is wearing a green, white and black tunic with a slash of saturated, matte eye-shadow in the exact same shade of green. Jeanne, who always dresses with stark chic, wows me with a yolk-yellow wrap and head-dress in heavy cotton.

'Oho, Jeanne!' I exclaim. 'Elegant!'

'You told me you wanted to see some traditional dress. Well.'

'Hello, Auntie, how are you?'

Uh-oh. Claude's feeling sociable too.

'I don't want to sit near you,' says the woman who was so good at analysing poetry the other week, looking at him severely through hooded eyes. 'I don't want too much talk-talk.'

He slinks away.

'How many divorces have you had?' she demands.

'I have had seven. It is important to be honest about these things,' he says silkily.

Crutches guy comes up to me.

'You know the black guy, with the dreadlocks, he told me yesterday that he dreamt about you.'

He's talking about Tejan.

'I'm sure he dreamt that he was in a very interesting class about writing,' I say.

Somehow, as the season has turned over, there's been a subtle, warm change and coalescence within the group, even though there are more extra people than ever and tensions are rising at expenses time. Part of their acceptance of me is, I'm sure, because I'm obviously the daughter of a migrant myself—a second generation British Asian. As the historian and biographer Caroline Moorehead writes, 'Like internally displaced people, like refugees, there have always been migrants. Ever since the sixteenth century, people have moved to work, to explore, to travel, to find better lives. What no one quite anticipated was the emergence of new multicultural societies, nor the new patterns migration has taken.'[7]

We continue with our poetry study and the students discuss the challenges of reading and writing it, explaining meaning and thought, grammar, brevity and structure.

'But what about the pleasures?' I ask.

'It brings you to the dream world out of yourself,' says Claude.

7 Caroline Moorehead, *Human Cargo: A Journey among Refugees* (London: Vintage, 2006), p. 283.

'Imagination. The sound of it when you say it. Rhythm,' say others.

'It makes you feel happy and sad,' says someone.

'How many more classes are there?' asks Don.

I have a few more classes here and also at the other centre in Victoria.

'Have you learnt anything?' I tease him. 'You can leave now if you like.'

He stays put while everyone ribs him and me and one another. Shady Kafele has written a piece which catches my attention for its detail and ring of truth. It's called 'The Army Barracks':

> Men and women march from one point to another, all wearing military fatigues. It's not just about guns, bombs and tanks inside: children are attending school, doctors and nurses work in the hospital, voices sing from the church. Football, basketball, volleyball and other sports take place inside the barracks.

'How do you know about barracks? Are you in the army?' I ask him.

He looks very cagey indeed.

'No, I, er, some of my folks have been in the army in, er, my country, and I've been over to visit them and seen, er, what it's all about.'

'Which is where?'

'In, er, in Malawi.'

'I'm asking because you have a proper London accent. You could be a guy from down my way.'

'Some of us are born here,' says someone to me rebukingly.

'I know that,' I reply.

'But also, people from East Africa, I have noticed, have very good English accents,' says someone.

'No. That is not true,' says someone else.

'OK. No more discussions about accents and nationality,' I say. 'This is a politics-free zone.'

But national and international politics are what brought us together, in this room, in this country. It's all-defining and inescapable and is reflected, in one way or another, in everything my students do, say or write. I have students from the two Congos, Cameroon, Malawi, Sierra Leone, Uganda, Burundi, Sudan, Iran, Syria, Ghana, Liberia and more. All these people's lives have been politicized by violence or violated by politics, or they wouldn't be here. They are all existing in reaction to what other groups' or governments' brutal power-playing—local, national or international, formal or informal, governmental or military, social or economic, rebellious or established, distant or close—has done to their home countries. And the way they're treated here is influenced by Europe's own political leaders' rhetoric, which both follows and reinforces media misrepresentation.

In his subsequent writing, Kafele refers to a romanticized vision of Africa, the kind you get in tourist brochures: 'Africa! Full of natural beauty, mountains, rivers and wildlife. Beautiful birds singing, snakes and tigers seem at peace.' He warns that the idealized image holds 'until you get down to the villages', where 'hungry malnourished children cry for food. Hopeless mothers, weary and hungry too, have nowhere to get food from. The sound of guns and bombs dominates the atmosphere. African leaders are busy destroying the beauty and the lives. Greed and divide and rule is the motivation. The money intended for the poor is used to unleash the pain.' He writes angrily that 'Africa is being destroyed by Africans with the help of the former colonies.'

Yet the continent's beauty is also genuinely yearned for by my African students. Beatrice has written about a place called Mukaziniro:

> I stand on this hill, looking at the view around me, far and wide. So many interlocking hills with gorge-like valleys in between, others with small terraces patched onto their slanting sides. And in between them, flat valleys and small houses with iron sheeting roofs dotted here and there. Beautiful.

In my students' work, memory and longing are always overlaid with pain and realism. Beatrice mentions that someone killed themselves on the Tube that morning, on the Jubilee Line at Swiss Cottage. She writes in class that it's reminded her of her cousin who hanged himself last year, 'I never attended his funeral. He was 30 years old. Why do they do it? I cry for the children they had or could have had, these suicides. I cry for them that they thought they couldn't bear it any more.'

We plod our way through a Shakespeare love sonnet which suddenly seems trivial and solipsistic compared with Malawian army life and the fallout from global conflict. I ask them what century Shakespeare wrote in.

'Nineteenth?'

'Nope.'

'Eighteenth? Seventeenth?' they call out.

'Sixteenth century,' I say. 'And what century did Tennyson write in?'

'Sixteenth?' is the immediate reply.

The fact is that English literature and its historic flashpoints are simply not that important at the moment, and that is completely understandable.

A little later, everything heats up, spills over and boils dry. An argument breaks out near my colleague, Hannah, who's giving out the travel expenses. For the last two weeks there haven't been enough expenses to go round as the group keeps growing. The newcomers do not even bother to pretend to be interested, pick up a pen, open an exercise book and write something. They just sit, waiting for the session to be over. I am tempted to bring in some money of my own, give it to them out of charity and then throw them out.

Who's doing the arguing in the expenses group? Why, it's Jeanne of course. She has a huge blow-out, crying, shouting and groaning. I remember that this is how she got into the group in the first place, even though she'd already done exactly the same course the previous year. She goes for the whole performance, face swollen, shouting in her dry, loud, berating voice, 'You are not giving me the money and I come every week, instead you give the money to the people who only come recently—and you see, someone came last week, and then this week she brought her two children and her husband, and another one brought her husband, so they can collect 16 pounds—and instead I come every week to work. But the new people don't do anything. They're not interested in the class, only in the money they can get. I'm asking you and you are ignoring me. It's because you don't see me!' She begins to shake and stamp her foot and moan and wheel about looking aggrieved. Her classmates are ignoring her. 'You don't see me! You don't see us!'

Quite the contrary, not only does Jeanne make herself extremely visible and audible, it's as though no one else is audible to her. It's interesting, though. She's confrontational, grating and awkward and yet a lot of what she's saying is damn right and everyone in the class had thought it but didn't say it. My colleagues and I realize that we should have registered names at the beginning of the course, limited the numbers and then set a budget.

Jeanne whirls round and appeals to me, suddenly abject.

'Can you help me?' she whines, holding out her hand and looking degradedly at my feet. In silent disgust, I give her eight pounds out of my own wallet.

Once she's got her money in her pocket, she calms down instantly. Her eyes are suddenly completely dry. The squalling performance is over and we can all breathe again. I puzzle over her, this strong woman who is simultaneously objectionable and admirable. In a quiet moment a little later, a volunteer comes to me and says, 'You know, we have "reserve funds" in the office upstairs—if anything like that happens again . . . you don't have to use your own money . . .'

I realize by her lack of surprise at what's been happening that this is normal. It was my own naivety about how people have to live and behave in the real world, just to survive, that made me baulk at it.

At the end of the class, I notice that things are changing in the lives of my regular students. They're beginning their year properly, striving and growing. Elodie, whom I had counselled about her interview at the Wallace Collection with little faith, comes up to me and says slowly, in rehearsed English, 'I have something to tell you. It is going . . . well!'

'It is?'

'I am on the training course for the museum.'

I give her an enormous hug of complete surprise and delight.

'Well done! You deserve it.' I jokingly add, 'It's because you are a wonderful, strong, confident person.'

And then beautiful Banyina approaches and says carefully, 'I have enjoyed your classes very much. But I will not be here next week.'

'Oh. All right. Will you be here the week after?'

'Ah. No,' she delicately replies, placing her hand upon my shoulder. 'I am going on a training course. Premiere Inn. I will travel and we will stay in a hotel, for the course.'

'Aha! Well! That is a very good reason.'

It's good to watch my new friends fly. But I wonder if I really taught them anything, or if they were just marking time, or if they expected me to teach them a particular thing and I failed to do so, or if anything I offered made any difference at all, or if we all just hung out in a room together and had a jolly time. Those who were good at writing—Beatrice, Jeanne, Kafele, Tejan, Claude—are still good, those who were poor haven't improved and those like Don or crutches guy who didn't feel comfortable writing in the first week still hadn't tried by the sixth.

After my class there's a singing group in the same room, which Jeanne and Beatrice are staying on for. They persuade me to stay too. Beatrice says in her thoughtful way, 'In life there are ups and downs and the way to deal with them is to rise above them and take opportunities, to accept chances and to make them a part of yourself. So, I sing and I welcome it very much.'

Jeanne says in her pushy way, 'It's a group for people who don't know how to sing, but they try to teach them to sing but they use it as a way to teach them really how to express themselves. I can sing and I am better than them but I go to help them, you know, just to help them . . .'

In the brief gap between my class and the singing group, Jeanne sits down and fills out a form.

'I am applying for funding to teach a sewing class here,' she says. 'We need sewing machines. If I get the funding, we will have just enough. Can I put you down as a reference?'

'Of course you can.'

In the sewing class, which Jeanne runs on Monday mornings, she wants to do a workshop on printed textiles, 'because African people don't know how to print'.

'I thought those printed wraps *were* African?'

'In some African countries, the wraps are national dress. In others, the prints are imported. And other African countries print and weave their own textiles—but not always with the traditional wax method,' she explains. 'But of course so many countries have now absorbed American fashions, so everyone looks American.'

I begin to get nervous about the singing group. Any of the six people who heard my unique reinterpretation of Madonna's 'Papa Don't Preach' in New York in 2003, when I was slow-clapped off the stage during my first and last public karaoke attempt, will know that I can't sing. Jeanne tells me firmly that it'll be fun: 'Recently we worked with a student who was doing his thesis, using the stories we told to make some music in his work. We had to create a song from scratch based on the first thing we saw when we came to England. He picked some of the people's stories and joined them all up to make a medley. It's funny, when we think of England, we think it's glamorous, we think it's nice. I told them, when I saw people, everyone was wearing black, it was sober, it was black and grey in the morning. And the ladies, the ladies they were wearing skinny jeans. And there was no style, *no style*. People wore the same things, skinny jeans, year after year. Another woman said she saw so many lights, lights everywhere at Heathrow Airport. Another one saw a red bus. Lots of red buses. Another one saw many many houses that all looked the same. And for me, the houses at Heathrow were zigzag shapes, all brown, and all the same, so I didn't know how to differentiate the houses and streets from each other, with zigzag shapes, and all dark. In my country the roofs are blue and green for those who live in trendy houses, but here everything's brown and dark and the same. So I was disappointed as there was no glamour. My sister had told me, "You're going to England? It's not beautiful." '

There are about eight of us in the singing group. It's led by a puckish Indian guy called Ashwin, who heaves out an electric keyboard and clunks it down at the front of the room with the cheerful words, 'Don't worry, they build us strong in India.'

'How long do these music classes go on for?' I ask.

'They're endless. They run every week,' says Jeanne.

As Ashwin sets up I begin to edge away, saying, 'I'll just sit in, over here. Ignore me. I have to write a report.'

'Oh, no no no, if you're in the room you're in the singing group. Now, up! Everyone in a semi-circle please,' says Ashwin.

He's a lively and inspiring teacher and is accompanied by a somewhat wilting English guy called Graham, who's an opera director. They're thinking of raising some money and putting together a show based on their work here. We talk briefly about collaborating, with music devised by Ashwin, the show arranged by Graham and the group members as a choir.

'We've got some funding to put on an opera later this year and we were talking about linking up with the writing group, maybe using some of the students' work,' says Graham.

'I'd love that,' I tell him, though I have little expectation that it'll happen given how stretched our resources are. 'We just did an In Memoriam—everyone wrote about their mothers. We could use those.'

Graham gets a little fluttery.

'Oooh! Well . . . I'm not sure I could handle that . . .'

'Oh no, no, no, no, no . . . it's totally positive, life-affirming,' I reassure him.

Ashwin gets us started on some nonsense songs and rounds to warm us up, then divides us into registers. I discover to my joy that I can still read sheet music. Jeanne has a ceiling-scrapingly thin, flaking soprano which she burbles away in, swaying and shaking her head with her eyes shut, regardless of what else is going on and whether or not we're singing a song. Beatrice has a dry, manly bass. I'm standing next to a man who has a very warm baritone. Ashwin shouts special encouragement to me, 'You're a tenor but you don't know it yet. You don't realize you're singing an octave below the other ladies. You can sing! You're holding the tune. You can't hear what I hear. When you hear your own voice, it's reflected off all the bones in your inner ear.'

He's very kind. He passes around the lyrics to the Beatles' 'All You Need is Love', by Lennon and McCartney.

'"Paul Ma-Car-Ran"?' says one of our group.

'Now, my parents *never* listened to music when I was growing up, which was in the 60s,' Ashwin's saying to himself as he tests the chords, 'which was the time you were supposed to be listening to the Beatles. So I know nothing about the Beatles. I'm learning now.'

The lyrics aren't too hard. Here are the first three lines:

Love, love, love
Love, love, love
Love, love, love

We screech up and down with the melody, gabbling and stumbling over the fast bits: 'Nothing you can make that can't be made. No one you can save that can't be saved. Nothing you can do but you can learn how to be you in time. It's easy!' Then, 'All you need is love! All you need is love—'

'And a visa,' sings Ashwin, 'and a place to stay, and some work, and someone who fills out forms correctly for you, and a friend who takes you places, and indefinite leave to remain, but hey let's pretend these lyrics are true, all together now!'

After we've petered out, Ashwin teaches us some new sounds with a stepping-up stepping-down melody. At first it sounds like a nonsense rhyme or a warm-up exercise, then Ashwin says, 'It's a Congolese folk song. I got it off the Internet.'

'Eh?' say all the Congolese students.

Ashwin takes out a piece of paper with the lyrics and tune on it. He shows it to us.

'Yeah, I was going to do a Congolese folk song and I was going to get you guys to show me how to pronounce it properly and we were going to do it together.' He looks around the group hopefully. 'You're from Congo, she's from Congo, he's from Congo. I was hoping that one of you was going to tell me what this meant.'

The group study it. There's a little moment of awkwardness and then, very tactfully, one of them says to him, 'There are so many Congolese languages. We're not to know if this is one or another.'

NEVERTHELESS, SOMETHING
Beatrice Tibahurira

Dear Joseph,

I am writing this letter to you but it's not for you alone. It's for all of my children. I am writing to you with the hope that you will pass this message on to your sisters Sandra and Ivy-Marie and your brothers Timothy and Jude. You are not my first born, nor are you my favourite child because I don't really have one. I like to think of you all as equal in my eyes.

I have chosen you because I think you will explain it best to the rest. This letter is an explanation of why I made the decision to leave you behind in Uganda and come to the UK to work. It was a hard decision to make but you were still young and I could never have explained to you then. Now that you are adults, I can.

To be able to do this, I will start from the beginning which is the year 1956 when I was born in Bugongi, Kabale. I will go through the 10 years I have been living in the UK, some of them working illegally and some of them depending on handouts from friends. What I have done and what I have gone through, what I could have done and why I stayed.

I am hoping that by the time you have read all this, you will not only know more about me but you will understand me and my shattered dream.

[*Beatrice breaks off, takes her pen, rewrites something and says to me, 'I've changed "shattered" to "unfulfilled". Shattered sounded too final. It's just one word but it makes a difference.'*

'And "unfulfilled" sounds more subtle,' I say. 'And the point is, you're not some victim who's been destroyed, you're a survivor.'

'Mm hmm. Yes I am. Does it mean I've stopped dreaming? No. I haven't.']

. . . you will understand me and my unfulfilled dream. Writing about it enables me to release something from within myself, something that cannot be touched or seen, that cannot be quantified, that is intangible. Nevertheless, something.

While you may understand me, you do not necessarily have to agree with me. You are an adult able to make your own observations, conclusions and decisions. I will be at peace with myself knowing that I have attempted to tell you all. To answer the unvoiced questions you must have had all along.

This letter, my son, could have been written by any of the millions of immigrants in the UK to their children, husbands, wives, relatives or friends they left behind. Some of us remained out of touch with them because either we cannot afford to get in touch or are embarrassed with the way we live here.

Now, here is my story:

I grew up in a close-knit family of parents, uncles, aunties and cousins. Our homestead is on a small hill we called Rwenzori after the Rwenzori Mountains in western Uganda.

I had two grandfathers: my father's father, baptised Ignatius, a name our people turned into Inyasio; and his younger brother named Rwanyina-Mariza, never baptised. They had one sister, my great aunt. All three never went to school. My great aunt was reputed to be a very hard-working girl. It was said that she raised her two brothers single-handedly after their parents died. For this reason she was a prize for any young man, hence the reason she married well. Her husband was a teacher from Muyumbu, three villages away. All her children went to school, guaranteeing a good future for them in 1940s and 1950s Africa.

On our side, life remained much the same as it had been when our grandfathers were children. The land we lived on belonged to my great-great-grandfather, who was named Kyorezo. It is on the left side of Bugongi, halfway to Mukaziniro. The road through our village is on the right side so a car could never drive up to our home. From the road, we had to walk down a steep path, past our well, then walk up a short valley to our homestead.

Both my grandfathers were Ababaize men. They made *ebitebe* (traditional stools), *eshekulo* (mortars) and *emihini* (pestles) for a living. We called them Ba Shwenhuru, meaning 'our grandfathers', only differentiating them by saying Shwenhuru Omuhuru (older grandfather) and Shwenhuru Omuto (younger grandfather).

It was common in our culture for men to have more than one wife, each wife with her own house on the same compound. The man rotated from one wife to the other. Usually two or three days in one house, then he would move to the next one. The days he was with a wife, he would go to dig with her in her garden (each wife had her own garden) or to harvest and he would cut the firewood for her. She was responsible for cooking for him, washing his clothes and giving him warm water to bathe. Women competed for favours from their husbands by trying to cook the best food or brew the best alcohol.

Bakiga men [the tribe Beatrice's grandfathers come from] were renowned for being fair to their wives and treating them equally but this was not always the case. While my older grandfather had four wives, his brother had three. My earliest memories are of my grandfathers living with their youngest wives only. The older wives were living each on their own in their round grass-thatched houses.

I was the firstborn of both my mother and my father [in a polygamous society]. My mother was 17 years old and my father was 19 when I was born. They had not attended school.

My mother was from Butobere, two villages away from Bugongi. Both her parents had died when she was young so I never got to know them. She and her two sisters Pulikeria and Lena and their brother John were raised by their older brother, George. Their eldest brother Samuel was already married when their parents died. My mother and her other siblings always maintained that Samuel's wife convinced him to relocate from Butobere to Maziba, 10 miles away, because they did not want to raise these children.

Samuel and George had had their own mother who had died, Pulikeria had her own mother who had gone away and Aunt Lena, Uncle John and my mother Plasidia had their own mother who was a much younger woman bought by my grandfather from a Rwandan family who were moving from Rwanda to central Uganda. She was from the Munyarwanda people. So many of them moved from Rwanda to Uganda in the 1930s, running away from the Hutu/Batusi ethnic war of that time. This woman also had an older daughter called Josephina who stayed with Aunt Lena, Uncle John and my mother but went away soon after the deaths of my grandfather and grandmother. She went to look for her Rwandan family.

Uncle John was the youngest of these children, being about two years old when their parents died. My mother was the second youngest. Uncle George was about 20 years old. He decided to stay with the young children, looking after them in every way, most of all by making sure that their land was not taken by poorer families. They owned about half of all the land in Butobere and if George hadn't been a responsible young man, that land would have been taken by other people and these young children would never have survived.

Their father had died suddenly without any earlier illness and their mother followed in childbirth within a month. They always said that their parents died of witchcraft. By the time I was born, they were all Christians and even though they believed that their parents died of witchcraft, none of them practised it.

Soon the children grew up and first Pulikeria then Lena and lastly my mother got married and moved away. By then John, the youngest, was at lower school. Like many families then, Uncle George had sent Uncle John to school simply because he was a boy. The girls never had a chance. Most people thought it was a waste of money to send girls to school as they would get married and take their knowledge to their new families.

Uncle George only married after his youngest sister, my mother, had married and left home. That is why I am older than his firstborn, Judith, even though George was much older than my mother. He died in 2011 aged 92. You attended his funeral in Butobere.

After his sisters were married off, John was persuaded by a friend to move from Kabale to Mbarara. This he did and got a job as a houseboy for the headmaster of Ntale school. He worked there until the headmaster, who was an Englishman, retired and moved back to England. By then, Uncle John had saved enough money to buy himself land. He bought it in Kyera village near Mbarara. He still lives there with his family today. My subsequent trips to his home in Kyera village always gave me a sense of belonging. I have never felt as welcome in any other home as I did in his. Even today when I call his daughters, my cousins, who are younger than me and do not really know me that well, we click so well it's as if we grew up together.

'What is a testimony? What is it to bear witness? What happens when we testify?'

It's my last day teaching in Bethnal Green. Winter's breaking at last and my students are happy and restless. In the clear Easter light they look at me with bright, impatient eyes.

'When you testify,' says Claude, 'you give an account of a history seen or lived through, experienced or witnessed. "I witnessed" or "I experienced" . . . witnessing is something you saw with your own eyes as it happened. Experiencing is something you lived through.'

'What is the first criterion for a testimony?'

'The most important thing is honesty: it must be a true account of events. Being there,' says Claude.

'Yes. "Witness" is both a noun and a verb. You can be a witness to an event, and you can witness something. "Testimony" is a noun, "to testify" is the verb. A testimony can be verbal or written.'

I find a half-dead board pen and write down everything we've said, remembering some riveting advice from another essay I read in preparation for the course. Here goes:

'Because most classrooms have a whiteboard, the ability to use one effectively is essential. [. . .] The size of the lettering is important—writing a few words and then checking legibility from all parts of the room is important [. . .] emphasising different points through colour can be very helpful.'[8]

'I witnessed a man of 50 years hit by a hit-and-run driver,' says Claude. 'He was half dead. I took down the registration details and told the police. They thank me a million times.'

'I witnessed something,' says Beatrice. 'I was on the bus, Ilford to Wood Green, and there was a BMW with the top down, driven by a black man, Jamaican I think, on the inside. The lights were red. The bus driver, he was white, he spat out of the window and it landed on the BMW driver's head. The BMW driver swore, parked his car blocking the bus, gets out and shouts and screams at the bus driver. All the other bus passengers ran away but I stayed because it was just so interesting. The police come and talk to everyone. The BMW driver says the bus driver spat on his head deliberately. The bus driver promises that he was just spitting casually and it landed on the man's head by accident. Eventually the bus driver apologized to the BMW driver. It was amicable.'

A very fleshy, quiet, thick-set guy in an army jacket, who only turned up today and seems extremely vulnerable,

8 Liz Dixon, Josie Harvey, Ron Thompson and Sarah Williamson, 'Practical Teaching' in James Avis, Roy Fisher and Ron Thompson (eds), *Teaching in Lifelong Learning: A Guide to Theory and Practice* (Maidenhead: McGraw-Hill International, 2009), pp. 119–42; here, p. 129.

says, 'I witnessed 9/11. I was in New York. I still think and write about it.'

As he talks, he wipes his face with a soft yellow T-shirt that's bunched on his desk, smelling it and rubbing it against his mouth like a baby with a comfort blanket.

'I wrote a book about Western imperialism in the Congo, five years of work. I sent it to a charity but I've heard nothing,' says Claude. 'I sent it to many people and they said it is too strong, change the title, change too much. But I have no sponsor. I phoned the charity last week, they said, "Oh, we are too busy, we don't know . . ."'

'Be careful. It's easy to be taken advantage of,' I say. 'I can give you advice on that but there's a proper way of doing it.'

'When I was at university studying music,' says Manny, 'me and my two friends, I was always together with them, we want to do a public-theatre course but it was the same time as our composition class. So we say to the composition teacher—we have a disease. A deadly disease. We fail the test for a deadly disease, so we can't come to composition class.'

'Now why don't you write all of that down?' I ask him.

He shakes his head.

'I could compose something to express how I feel. Music,' he says.

At break, during the expenses scrum, I make a mistake so vulgar and thoughtless that I can barely write it down. I have brought in a big selection of new books, fiction and non-fiction, just for Beatrice. More than 20, a bagful, all recently published. It's my tribute to her dedication and talent but of course it's the wrong thing to do. I try to give the bag to her at the end of break but everyone immediately notices and gets angry.

'What have you got there?' says someone loudly.

I can't say this is a private present, not a class handout, because I shouldn't be making private presents in the first place. I let go of the bag and step back, hot, awkward and caught out. Beatrice's face has gone all closed and discreet.

'We should all have some. We should all look,' they say, riled and aggressive.

They are right. I should have brought in a book for everyone or waited until the course was over, made a tea date with Beatrice for another time and place and given them to her then, as a friend.

'Of course . . . please . . . pardon me . . . they're all . . . for everyone,' I say faintly into their outraged faces.

Keeping her eyes down, Beatrice takes all the books out of the bag, turns them over to glance at the covers and passes them along without a word. Everyone grabs the books and they soon disappear, even into the hands of those who don't care about books and don't read books and don't want books. I am too embarrassed to look anywhere.

All the books are now out of sight. I implore the class to make use of the last minutes we have.

'Today's the last day, no writing, no money, so write,' says Banyina chirpily to Don, who's scratching his chin over his still-completely-empty exercise book. I'm struck by a comment like that coming from her, another favourite of mine, until I realize that she too has not written a single thing during the course, merely been voluble, charming, funny and gorgeous. She half-winks at me and dances in her seat.

We get down to an exercise and the room is thick with concentration for a few minutes. A sharply dressed guy I've never seen before walks straight into the room and beckons to me, hard eyed, cocking his hand. I assume he works for the centre and think there might be an emergency, so I leave the room for a moment. We stand together on the landing, just outside the swing doors.

'Hello?' I say.

The guy's standing too close, grinning down hard into my face.

'Who are you? What are these classes?'

'They're writing workshops.'

'I will take your details—you can introduce me to some way of getting published,' he says, so charmlessly fake-charming that my stomach turns over.

'You could try English PEN. We're working on a booklet—'

He snorts with derision, his body gives a stiff twitch of irritation and his expression gets surly.

'Huh! If you google English PEN, my name comes up.'

I doubt that.

'What is your name?' I ask him.

'Jean-Louis. Jean-Louis is my name.'

As he says his name, lips curling sumptuously over the syllables, his face softens and glows with delight. He actually turns his gaze up to the sky like a special sunflower planted by God.

'What is your phone number?' he asks me harshly.

'I can't give you my phone number because I work at a radio station and I can't answer my phone in the studio.'

'Then you can introduce me to the BBC,' he says, smiling menacingly, this slick guy in sharp, cheap clothes and long, square-toe pimp shoes, looking me straight in the eye, occasionally touching my arm when he talks, playing me hard.

'No. I'm not going to do that and I need to get back to my class.'

His face and body language change completely and he snarls and tuts in anger and disgust. He steps back sharply, looking at me in open derision, turns on his heel and marches away, feet clicking hard on the ground.

Being a displaced person, I realize, watching him go, doesn't suddenly make you *not* a nasty, arrogant jerk who bullies women. Thank goodness there's no one like that in my class.

I go back into the room. As the exercise is ending and we prepare to say our goodbyes, I whisper to Beatrice, mortified, 'I am so, so sorry. It was a mistake to do that. That was the wrong thing to do. I shouldn't have handed you the books like that. Did you get any?'

'I got two.'

'Give me your address and I'll send you something.'

She hesitates for a moment.

'I am in temporary accommodation.'

Again—stupid of me—I should have thought. Beatrice gives me an address in South London, care of a friend. I promise to write up her work and see what I can do with it and then, somehow, the clock hand has sped to the final minutes.

My students are boisterous and affectionate. They ask me if I'll be coming back that summer and I say it's unlikely. One student tells another, 'No, Andrew will be doing the lessons.'

'Andrew? Who is this Andrew?' I joke. 'Forget about Andrew!'

I thank them for being so welcoming, so entertaining and so lively and wish them all the best. We hug, shake hands and say daffy things to one another. But they are keen to get on with the rest of their lives. Manny jiggles my hand in his huge, dry, pleasant one and whispers to me, 'I am a teacher. I know a teacher when I see one.'

Then Kafele stands up straight, his eyes shining a little, and says, 'We wish you the best. *We* wish you.'

We say goodbye.

That evening is also my last at the centre in Victoria, where my students are coming along in their own capable fashion. They are not in deep need of any help at all. I had forgotten to mention that here, in the South London centre, even the snacks are of a more plentiful and expensive variety. In Bethnal Green we have a little sponge cake or a butterscotch biscuit; in Victoria there is heating, light, cleanliness, cheerful decor, fresh fruit including tight neon-orange satsumas and bubbling bunches of grapes, long rolls of fancy biscuits, juice, drinks, crisps, thick fresh paper, good pens.

The lesson plans for the centre in Victoria have been following those of Bethnal Green, with a slight lag. As my students mull over the meaning of poetry, I gaze at the walls, where WELCOME is written in 16 different languages and 7 different scripts, next to a sign saying *Every child matters.* On a poster are the words *Be Healthy, Stay Safe, Enjoy and Achieve, Make a Positive Contribution, Achieve Economic Well-Being.* There are shelves for general books and bilingual books.

'Poetry is an emotional feeling put onto paper,' says my hip Japanese student.

'But it must also have verses—style—structure,' says an American woman.

'No idea, no meaning, structureless,' says Victor, our shy-but-droll Latin American 60-something, gloomily, shaking his head. He had told me earlier that his goal was to 'integrate into English life'.

'But this isn't "English" life,' I said, gesturing around at the group, but also meaning London in all its variety.

'But it is reality,' he philosophically replied.

'The form of a poem helps to structure your thoughts. You refine, choose the best bits, edit, discipline it, skin it down. The limitations give you freedom,' I say.

We attempt some verses.

'In a wedding pair, the bride is . . . the woman?' asks Tünde, my twinkle-eyed Hungarian student. She's in her late 50s or early 60s.

'Yup. And the man is the groom.'

Tünde writes about fresh spring blossom on a tree, 'white flowers stuck together, a bride standing over me.'

'In my language, Persian,' remarks Sahar, one of the lovely sisters, 'we have rules that we all know. The end of every sentence ends in a certain way—it matches the ends of the other sentences.'

My Japanese student Mitsuo's parents, who're probably still poring over his 16-page coming-out letter, are obviously much on his mind. He writes me a lovely, simple but clever six lines:

A boy leaves home to live independently.
His parents give him money,
'To buy nice food.'

A boy is getting married, his parents are retired.
He gives them money,
'To buy nice food.'

But the gentle poetry chat is interrupted by one of my older students, who lives in a very built-up area in town and wants to tell us about the crime he just witnessed: 'I have heard between 5 to 9 murders in the last 10 years. Including up until last Sunday when I was walking on the street when two men shot at each other. A woman between them fell, a crowd gathered and they'd gone to help her while I ran away a hundred yards and peered up like a meerkat. When I looked, a woman sat with the shot woman's head on her lap and another woman knelt beside her to help. Six police cars came in the space of two minutes. I like London for the speed of its police. And when I look at the scene of crime, they came from north *and* south. A helicopter hovered above. Next day I learnt on the news that the helicopter was an air ambulance to take her to be treated in the hospital.'

'Have the people who were shooting been caught?' the rest of the group asks.

'Not yet. In my area, I need eyes like a fly—a thousand eyes—at the front and back.'

'What do you think it was to do with?' I ask.

'Drugs and gangs. Always.'

This man is a community organizer himself and says the situation hasn't improved in his decade in the borough. Delicate Marie Lavoile, clearly much affected by this anecdote, has let it bleed into the springtime ode I asked them to write:

'Everything is touched with fear, a flush of terror.

The trees are bare, making room for new ones.'

We talk about the parts of London that we live in. Tünde says she lives in Leyton, near the 2012 Olympic site, and that a group of anti-capitalist protestors held some demonstrations there. She asked them about some other events they were holding: 'I went to their talk at Trafalgar Square in favour of socialist communism. I said to the guy, "Have you ever lived in a socialist country? I have. It's not nice."'

'What did the guy say?'

She rolls her eyes.

'He had nothing to say. He gave me a book on Marx and a newspaper cutting. Marx is very popular here,' she says drily.

We have only a few minutes of the class left. Despite the physical comfort of the room and the like-mindedness of the group, it has been a less interesting, less meaningful course. A pastime, not a lifeline. Still, it's impossible to predict what affects people. Months later, Mitsuo emails me to say, touchingly but mysteriously, 'That workshop connected between myself and a lot of people.' He, in his young 20s, from Japan, asks to use one of Tünde's poems in an art performance event he's doing at the Tate Modern. Tünde, in her 50s or so, from Hungary, goes along and hands out paper copies of the poem for people to read while he performs. They wouldn't have met had it not been for the workshops.

DIFFERENTLY BEAUTIFUL

Beatrice Tibahurira

On my father's side, both his parents lived to a ripe old age, my grandmother outliving my grandfather and all people of their generation. She was believed to be a hundred years old when she died. She had been a small woman of about five feet. She was also very [light] brown, in fact as brown as a mixed-race person, almost like a white person.

My grandmother's real age was not known but just guessed. She always told us of the drought that hit Central Africa at the turn of the nineteenth and twentieth centuries. She was a young girl then, who had just started her menstrual periods. Her mother had given birth to 14 children. Her parents and 11 of her siblings, nephews and nieces all died due to the drought. She survived with one sister and one brother.

She told us horrifying stories of how her family, neighbours and animals died as the survivors looked on helplessly. How they buried those who died at first but in the end did not even try to bury them as they had no energy at all. They simply covered the dead bodies with dry grass and walked away. How they went hungry and thirsty for days on end, walking long distances to get any green leaves to eat or water to drink.

I always held her in awe and respect. Because of what she had gone through, she swore these words: *enjara ribi*, meaning the bad, terrible hunger, or *eizooba ribi*, meaning the terrible sun that shone and shone on and on and on. She had lost many people in this drought, so if she said these words, it meant she was very serious about whatever she was telling us to do or not to do. She did not use them often and as children she could actually command us with them. It was as if something bad would happen to us if we disobeyed. I always did what she wanted me to do.

We called her Mukaka, simply meaning Grandmother. She had been baptized Bridget but our people had turned it into Birizita. They did this to most Christian names because they found them hard to pronounce. On the other hand, my grand-father called her Keigamirwa, a pet name meaning 'My rock' or 'I lean on her' or 'She supports me'. Most men had pet names for their wives and vice versa. To me, both my grand-father and my grandmother looked old but the story was that she was older than him and that she had actually been the one who proposed to him. This was inappropriate in our culture; it was always the man who proposed. Even my elder cousin, Ferry, who told me this, was whispering when he said it, so I knew automatically that I must keep mum about it. But inside me, I admired her for having had such courage. She was such a survivor and it went without saying that she was the cleverest person on our hill as people always consulted her about various issues. To me, she seemed to know everything. That was when my world was my family, relatives, village and surrounding vil-lages, only a few hundred people.

Even today, after knowing that the world is vast, with mil-lions of people with all levels of knowledge, I still think of her when I am going through a bad patch, knowing she would have had an answer for any nagging questions I may have. Sometimes I say aloud, 'Mukaka, what should I do in this case?' Knowing full well that she is not here to give me the answer.

She loved me and I loved her to bits. It was widely known and accepted that I was her favourite grandchild. She was my grandfather's first wife. He had three other wives, one of them younger than my own mother. The story was that when my aunt, who was older than my father, got married, a dowry was paid for her in the form of cows and goats. My grandfather decided to get a new, younger wife for himself and wanted to pay for her using my aunt's dowry. His wife, my grandmother, decided that this could not happen and ordered my father to look for a girl to marry so my grandfather could pay for her with the cows—this is how my mother came into the picture. But my grandfather decided that even if he couldn't use my aunt's dowry to pay for the dowry on a new wife for himself, he would use other resources. So he did this and brought in and married the woman who was younger than my mother.

My village, Bugongi, is a typical village like any other in Kabale district. It is a district widely known for its beauty with many interlocking hills, some very steep, others slanting gently. In some areas it has gorge-like valleys and in others small plateaus or mini hills. It also has some stretches of flat land like where Kabale town stands.

Most homesteads are built on the plateau, the flat valleys or the lower parts of the slanting hills. The rest of the hills are almost all cultivated by using small terraces so as to prevent soil erosion. This makes the scenery very beautiful. Kabale district is in the south-western corner of Uganda, with Congo to the west and Rwanda to the south. Both countries are famous for gorilla tracking. This makes Kabale a route for tourists going to either of them.

Bugongi is really a suburb of Kabale town. Approached from Kabale town, it is a large valley, narrowing as you go further. Mukaziniro is the furthest part of Bugongi and is where the two hills on either side of the valley meet. Mukaziniro means 'a place for dancing'. The view round it is scenic, hills and valleys. Some hills look as if they are embracing each other and some valleys look as if they are tunnels entering and disappearing into the hills.

Mukaziniro is a marketplace now and is often used for political meetings and rallies. In the old days, it was a place where people congregated to celebrate the sorghum harvest in July and August. Sorghum is the most important grain food for the Bakiga.

Mukaziniro is a feel-good place where people hold meetings, exchange gifts, sell or buy food, drink and dance. I have lovely memories of dancing and playing at Mukaziniro in the open with the African sun hot on us but with the breeze that is characteristic of hilltops in Kabale making it pleasant. The green valleys below us, the terraced hills, some with people digging, small houses or homesteads here and there roofed with white iron sheets, or round grass-thatched huts. Cattle and goats grazing on the hillsides, even on steep cliffs. A car, a lorry or a pick-up carrying goods tied with ropes, its load looking much bigger than the vehicle itself, with a film of dust following it on the narrow road and we children claiming it as our own if we saw it first. 'That is mine,' I would shout and it would be mine until it got out of sight, no one would try to claim it again. Life was so uncomplicated, so differently beautiful!

CHAPTER EIGHT

NOGGIES, NOGGIES, NOGGIES

In the months that follow, English PEN puts together a sleek monochrome anthology of material from all the groups it's been working with over the last six months. I sort through my notes, submit some of my students' work and write the introduction to the anthology, which is called *Big Writing for a Small World*:

> In the autumn of 2011 and the spring of 2012 a small group of London writers and poets encountered a host of new worlds. [. . .] Through seemingly small exercises, brief writing assignments, short essays and on-the-spot writing challenges we uncovered great swathes of recent history, learned about long journeys undertaken, losses endured, challenges fought, gambles made with life and death, wars witnessed, loved ones lost and regained. I can't speak for the other writers but I can say that I learned much more from my students than they could possibly have learned from me.

> Our enterprise was entitled Big Writing for a Small World. What we found, instead, was small but powerful writing, by seemingly ordinary (but secretly extraordinary) people, which enabled us

to discover the bigness of the world and the laser power of mere words. The sessions were by turns hilarious, heartbreaking, inspiring and baffling: I am still confused about the 'noggies' that form the subject of a Hungarian student's poem. So I will end this introduction not with any solemn words of greatness about the triumph and resilience of the human spirit but with a writerly enquiry to my pupil, Tünde Molnár: what on earth are noggies?[9]

In the collection is a striking piece of writing by a woman from another group. The woman, Haimanot Nasser, from Sudan, describes her fourth (and finally successful) attempt to enter the UK, hidden in a lorry under piles of boxes containing chocolates and sweets. There was no air to breathe, no room to move and her hands and feet went numb. When the police came to check the lorry, the migrants had to cover their faces with plastic to stop the sniffer dogs smelling them. Haimanot writes, 'I lost my father and my family, but now I have freedom.'

I wish I could have submitted the art exercises my Bethnal Green group did one morning, when they drew themselves and one another. Needless to say, it descended into chaos, with people shielding their faces in an attempt not to be drawn and then complaining (jokingly) about the results. Jeanne gave me a picture of the most beautiful lady goddess ever to grace the galaxy, so much so that I asked, in sparkling wonder, 'Who's that?'

'It's me.'

'Oh!'

Some reactions are impossible to hide. Fragile Rose, who was so worried about her perfect English, did a soft pencil sketch of a clear little face looking anxious, eyes wide, mouth open. Beatrice drew herself as an unrecognizable, glaringly angry head with staring eyes, like a thunder god from a totem pole. Friendly Elodie, currently showing unsuspecting members of the public around the Wallace Collection, drew a classmate of hers, a smiling young Asian woman who had not uttered a single peep for the entire course. Next to the drawing, Elodie wrote about her friend, 'I am shine [shy] but I am happy to be here. I am Nurgahan.' Manny naughtily sketched Jeanne, drew a love heart on her front and a halo around her head and wrote, 'I lovy Jeanne.' Glorianna, with a typically strong pen hand, created a striking image of a woman with her arms crossed across her front, a crucifix swinging askew from her neck. Tejan did a funny cartoon strip featuring pretty accurate caricatures of famous dictators—Mu'ammer Gaddafi and Robert Mugabe were both in there—with the caption 'African Dictators Love Glasses'. True enough, they were all in specs. He also wrote, kindly, 'Big Writing for a Small World. I learned. I discovered. I think about writing.'

Kafele, for some reason, drew Michael Jackson in a fluffy angora jumper. Later, though, I found some of his writing deep in the pages of the exercise book he'd given back to me. There was a lurid memory of a childhood trip:

Many years ago in Timbuktu I witnessed a magician transforming himself into a snake. And then there was another walking on a rope while stabbing himself with a dagger.

And then another recollection:

Back in the days in Timbuktu I saw a man who was supposed to be a paramount chief being accused by the military of being an enemy of the state, somebody they called a rebel. So I witnessed the army laid him on the ground and he was butchered and after that I saw them removing his internal organs. And I felt very traumatised and so much horrified.

These are the things that none of my students mentioned outright but wrote about in the pieces they gave me, untitled and unannounced, or left for me to discover. It is events like these that form the unsaid background, the unspoken feeling—the uncomposed music, as Manny would have it—to our lessons.

It takes nearly a year for me to write this book. My students are off living their lives, one step forward at a time. One evening I am speaking at an event about my work in prisons and I get a lovely surprise—my Hungarian student Tünde Molnár is there, grinning at me from the audience. We hug and catch up.

'What are you doing now?' I ask.

'Well, you know I work in the library at a university? I want to do a poetry cafe there—some writers, some readings, a little food. I told my boss and he said, "Well, you must study for it."'

'Study what?'

'Hospitality and Management. So, two days a week, I go, and if I continue for one more year, I get a Master's degree. It's good, at 54, to be a student again, going to the British Library. And I get time to write. Now, I have something for you.'

She reaches into her bag and produces a white booklet, carefully spiral-bound, with plastic covers. I look at the title and burst out laughing.

Noggies

To My Lost Family's Matters

'You asked what noggies were. Turn to the first page,' says Tünde.

'"To Bidisha. What on earth are Noggies? Noggies is a message word of my generation of fifties. Noggies means soft and sentimental. Noggies wants to tell the world that this soft and sentimental generation has a great past and a great future,"' I read out.

When I study the booklet later my skin chills at the sharpness and brilliance of the writing. Tünde has produced a full poetry collection, beautifully worded, beautifully written, a vivid family history in beloved items. Each poem is a precise snapshot reaching from the deep past into the present—together, they tell a generations-old story.

The first poems commemorate her great-grandfather. 'Noggies to My Great-Grandfather's Soldier Picture' recalls 'the brown frame paper holding a bygone history, hard brown photo glued on hard board paper'. The next, 'Noggies to My Great-Grandmother's Singer Sewing Machine', describes the 'strong metal legs [. . .] holding the wheel and the pedal' and depicting the machine as 'a cradle of the clothes' dream [. . .] a factory giving jobs to my family during the century, a member of each family during their life'. As she describes them, I see the fragile brown photograph and the sturdy black sewing machine.

'Noggies to My Great-Grandmother's Bible' describes a house, long before radio and TV, where the kitchen was the most important room, just a cupboard, a fireplace and chairs around the table, on which the Bible always lay on the right, close to the door. Her great-grandmother's last wish was to be laid to rest with her Bible but, Tünde writes, 'still today I see her Bible and her words when I look at the right side of her kitchen table.'

Tünde's grandmother kept 'an embroidered French-style velvet case' containing wavy iron hair slides that gave her a 1930s flapper hairdo. She worked in a cinema in the late afternoons and was inspired by the chic 'boardwalk looking, flapper hairstyle, millinery appearance' of the actresses. Her wave clips were used every day and 'sculpted her hair in lazy big waves' just like the stars. Tünde writes, 'The rust ate my grandmother's iron hair wave clips and they disappeared during the family history.'

Through her words I see her entire family, artistic and cultured like her, with a hint of humour in the eye and a quirky love of particular things. She describes a wooden tobacco box of her grandfather's, with a cigarette engraved on the lid and compartments for the cigarette papers and loose tobacco inside, and his love of a twilight drink in the family courtyard:

> My grandfather enjoyed the protocol of using his
>   soda siphon.
> First he took a long soda glass.
> He poured a small cool white wine in it and lifted
>   the soda siphon above the glass.
> He slowly pushed the handle of the siphon and
>   the soda shot out straight into the glass.
> The water falling, became calm and formed
>   bubbles,
> The bubbles mixed with the wine.

There are noggies for the round table made by her father, a master joiner who decreed that 'where there is no table, there is no family' and believed a round table 'makes you practise equality . . . face to everybody's face'; and there are noggies for his Sokol-branded transistor radio, which he queued for in a shop for hours and operated using 'the small handle and the long one'. Tünde describes her mother's porcelain crockery set as wearing 'festive dress' because it was stored in a cupboard whose shelves were lined with lace-edged tissue. The soup plates had purple roses and the flat plates had blue lilies painted on them. She describes the old market that began so early that the moon and stars still shone even as the sun rose. The smell of fruits and vegetables cut the air and their colours cut the light: 'coral red carrots, blood red tomatoes, spring green lettuces,

forest green beans, olive green cucumbers, yellow green cab-
bages'. Tünde writes, 'Now they are ancient stories and I'm
the only keeper of those memories.'

The evocation of these beautiful things comes to a
screeching halt with the 'Noggies to My Brother's Flared
Trousers', with its cautionary subtitle: 'From 1970'. The subject of this poem is some 'stupefyingly hilarious idiosyn-
cratic trousers, wide forming large bell-bottom pants'
coloured—get this—'white, light grey, light blue and dark
blue stripes', which her brother kept in a special section of
his wardrobe and put on in a Saturday-night ritual while he
sculpted his hair and 'disco music sprayed around the room'.
The last line of the poem is 'How happy I was. I had a
brother in 1970.'

The next poem, 'Noggies to My Brother's 37 Dreams',
is a numbered list. First is 'To be young.' The second is, 'To
grow up endlessly smiling.' At 14, it's 'To build the future.'
At 15, 'To struggle for peace.' At 16, 'To stop the violence.'
The numbers go up. Then:

31. To stop the dictatorship.
32. To stop the dictatorship.
33. To stop the dictatorship.
34. To stop the dictatorship.
35. To stop the dictatorship.
36. To stop the dictatorship.
37. To stop the dictatorship.

My brother was 37 when he died in the dictatorship.

CHAPTER NINE

AS FAR AWAY FROM DEATH

I am writing this on New Year's Day 2013. I love the silent week as Christmas ends and the year turns over and slips forward. I've written to Beatrice at the last address I had for her and received no reply yet. Reading through the last scraps of my students' work and combining them with the self-descriptions they gave me at the beginning of the year, I think of them as leading puzzle-box lives, magic-box lives, small on the outside, big on the inside, like optical games from the Museum of Childhood. Behind the stereotype, the ignored face or quickly forgotten name is an individual who has experienced world-spanning journeys, stark opposites, vast distances and differences, dramatic upheaval, extreme change, new things to be learnt quickly, past things to be grieved over, horrors to recall, lost things yearned for, the devastation and forced rebuilding of identities and lives. My students are much more than just figures who pass unnoticed on the street, looking as though they've walked for miles: the tired woman with bags of shopping on the bus; people waiting in queues, looking shifty and cold and out of place; the cleaners, porters and janitors who're ignored by office workers; the till operators and security guards awake and working in the middle of the night; the unseen hands, unnamed individuals and unremembered faces in hospitals, nurseries, care homes, factories. As Maeve Sherlock, former chief executive of the Refugee Council, writes:

> The reality of refugee movements is an accumulation of personal stories played out against the backdrop of international conflict and persecution around the world. But in our media the stories only start on the day refugees step onto British soil. In film parlance, refugees have no 'backstory'. They are seen only as supplicants needing our help, while the story of what they fled and the courage they may have shown in escaping it are invisible. There is not even a reference to their past lives, no sense that today's refugees were yesterday simply mothers, brothers, children, doctors, teachers, builders, often ordinary people to whom extraordinary things happened.[10]

My students have grown up in normal homes in vibrant communities, have had jobs and families and lives, only to see those things destroyed by war, corruption, abuse, persecution and fear. They flee violence or poverty, seek sanctuary or a better life and then encounter the most disheartening aspects of a new country: unsympathetic governments, a disbelieving and suspicious society, prisons, detention centres, destitution, further abuse, exploitative employers,

---

10 Maeve Sherlock, Foreword to Edie Friedman and Reva Klein, *Reluctant Refuge: The Story of Asylum in Britain* (London: British Library, 2008), pp. ix–x; here, p. ix.

cultural ignorance, violence. They are kept alive by their own survival abilities and others' altruism and by a fragile system of underfunded charities, meagre welfare and stretched resources. From the traumatic immensity of what has gone before, their days are eaten up by the details of bare existence: working out the bus system and finding money for a bus ticket; trying to learn languages and get a foothold in a new country; needing to be taken everywhere; filling in forms; trying to get a phone, a safe bed, identification papers, representation and advocacy, a place to learn, teach, study, sleep or work.

Though their current lives feel small to them and the losses, limitations and injustices of both now and then cut deep, my students' world is huge. They speak multiple languages, have passed through multiple countries, crossed multiple borders. We should be listening to them, not silencing them, because we have much to learn. As journalist Robert Winder writes in his book *Bloody Foreigners*: 'Each migration was an adventure: indeed, it is amazing how often an immigrant's journey closely resembles a heroic escape—risky boat rides, midnight treks, cars nosing through dark woods, disguises, the barking of police dogs, hiding places, secret papers, close shaves, nail biting escapes and whispers. Yet we habitually see immigrants not as brave voyagers but as needy beggars.'[11]

Each piece written by my students is a plait twisting together the past, the present and the future, despair and

11 Robert Winder, *Bloody Foreigners: The Story of Immigration to Britain* (London: Little, Brown, 2004), p. 3.

hope, horror intertwined with trepidation, courage and determination. Behind every leaflet offering help at the Bethnal Green centre are thousands of unique and individual people who are in a strange place and need help, not an 'influx' or a 'deluge' or a 'wave' of immigrants. Behind every offer of counselling on a faded poster are myriad causes of grief. And behind the grief are abuse and injustice of one kind or another, or several together: sexual, political, military, economic, religious.

The people who come to Praxis are displaced and vulnerable, but these terms cover many different types of experience. Not all have been refused the right to stay in the UK and there are many different people at varying stages of the process of regularizing their lives. Asylum seekers are those who have applied for the right to be recognized as refugees. If their claim is successful, they require advice about what their rights are and how to exercise them, before they can begin to feel that their lives are their own and to set about fulfilling their potential, re-establishing themselves in the world instead of floating around in limbo, as Claude put it on our first day. Once their immigration status has been established and they are granted leave to remain, they must pass through several hurdles: finding housing, getting financial help, gaining employment or training and accessing health care (including mental health care and trauma counselling) and education. Edie Friedman and Reva Klein note in *Reluctant Refuge* that 'One area of improvement for refugees today is in the attention paid to their psychological needs. It provides a stark contrast with previous generations of refugees, most notably Holocaust survivors, who were discouraged from talking about their horrific experiences.'[12]

However, this support is being offered in a general context of extreme social stigma, public hostility, cultural ignorance and political complacency at best, antipathy at worst. The clichés are that migrants (with no distinction between types of migrant) are opportunistic, backward, grasping advantage-takers who want to 'steal' either British jobs or British welfare benefits, who are involved in organized crime at least and terrorism at most, cannot be bothered to learn English, are lying about where they have come from, what happened to them and why they came to Britain, are going to sully and warp English values, do not want to integrate and are trying to play the system for university places (which they will then try to stretch into permanent leave to remain), free houses, easy employment and free health care.

Looking through the Bethnal Green centre's last few annual review publications, I am struck by the way its tone of pride in what the centre can provide is undercut by wariness about the wider political and economic context. In the last year, more than 13,000 people signed in at this centre. The year before, it was more than 12,000. The year before, 14,000. Vaughan Jones, the centre's chief executive, writes in the 2009–10 review that he is 'fearful of the future and our capacity to achieve our ambitions. We are at the start of a radical realignment of public services which will have a tremendous impact on the communities [helped by the centre].' He continues, 'The one thing we must not let

12 Friedman and Klein, *Reluctant Refuge*, p. 29.

happen in these difficult times is for the creativity and drive which migration brings to wither and for talent to be wasted.' A year later the tone is more alarmed, the news worse. Jones writes that 'in straitened economic times, migrants become easy scapegoats. [. . .] The pendulum has swung far into the red and whilst as always this report records and highlights [the centre's] many achievements, it does so in a very bleak landscape.'[13]

At the moment, more than 40 organizations are working for the Still Human Still Here campaign to end the destitution of refused asylum seekers. These are people who have fled persecution, been refused asylum, exhausted all rights to appeal and find themselves with nothing—no housing, no benefits, no money to buy food. At the moment, over 200,000 refused asylum seekers are living destitute. Women are especially vulnerable to sexual violence and sexual exploitation in these circumstances. The charity Women for Refugee Women, whose director is the writer Natasha Walter, is one of the organizations involved in the campaign. On their website is the testimony of a woman named Herlinde Lokkuke, whose asylum case was rejected several times. She was made destitute. She writes:

> When you are destitute you come across people like you with many different stories. Women like myself who have nowhere to go and spend their nights in shelters. Sometimes those shelters are full

---

13 Vaughan Jones, Introduction to Praxis Community Projects, *Annual Review, 2009–10* (London: Praxis Community Projects, 2010), p. 2.

and women are forced to spend the night on the streets. One woman told me how she had been raped on the streets because she was sleeping rough. Some women go to Heathrow Airport to sleep or they take a night bus, going around and around the streets of London.[14]

She adds that some women are forced to become prostitutes to survive and I know from my own research that, in addition to this, many others find themselves in serial abusive, coercive set-ups where they have to give sexual labour or provide other work (like cleaning and childcare) in exchange for shelter.

In the last year the reduction in public services, the removal of access to legal aid in many immigration cases, reductions in local authority and National Health Service spending, changes in benefits rules and regulations and the reduction in funding for voluntary groups and charities have all impacted on the country's poorest people and on the possibility of community-based support for them. In the 2011–12 report for the Bethnal Green centre, Jones writes, 'In the country of origin you are a citizen, in the new country your status as a human being is less clear.'[15]

---

[14] Women for Refugee Women, 'Herlinde's Story'. Available at: http://www.-refugeewomen.com/index.php/resources/stories (last accessed on 7 January 2014).

[15] Vaughan Jones, Introduction to Praxis Community Projects, *Annual Review, 2011–12* (London: Praxis Community Projects, 2012), p. 2. Available at: http://www.praxis.org.uk/information-and-resouces-page-7.html (last accessed on 7 January 2014).

Once a year, the centre holds a festival called New Voices, which is attended by thousands of Londoners and showcases the culture and diversity of the people it works with. It has music, dance, poetry, drama, kids' stuff, stalls and food and it's for everyone. Although I like the freshness of the name New Voices, I feel that these songs, these stories, have been going on for ever. Despite this, the prejudices haven't changed much, because people are not listening. Their prejudices are making them deaf. The voices have been speaking, singing, lamenting pain and also celebrating strength for a long time but they are ignored or disbelieved. Despite this, I believe in the power of testimony to touch people, much more than facts and figures do. Former Labour minister Barbara Roche is even proposing a British museum of migration, a bit like Ellis Island in America. *Migrant Voice*, which aims to present 'alternative positions on migration', debunk myths about immigration and counteract stigmatization and negativity, says pointedly that 'A migration museum would also cover British emigration: 5.5 million British nationals are estimated to be living abroad, roughly the same number as foreign nationals living here.'[16]

As I write, award-winning playwright Cora Bissett's musical *Glasgow Girls* is showing in Scotland after its premiere in London. It's based on the true story of a Kosovan girl, Agnesa Murselaj, who was deported with the rest of her family from a block of high-rise flats in Glasgow in the middle

---

16 *Migrant Voice*, 'Wanted: funder for UK "Ellis Island" Migration Museum, *Migrant Voice* 1 (2012), p. 1. Available at: http://migrantforum.org.uk/wp-content/uploads/full-MV-paper.pdf (last accessed on 4 January 2014).

of the night. Agnesa's friends from Drumchapel High School mounted a campaign to protest her detention, highlight the poor treatment of failed asylum seekers and raise awareness as more children from the school were dawn-raided, deported and detained.

Meanwhile, Women for Refugee Women has worked on several projects in which refugee women in the UK depict their experiences in their own ways. *Home Sweet Home* is a photography and testimony exhibition featuring images taken by women of their daily lives: the empty grey streets; the sinister and dirty accommodation; the cruelty, abusiveness and impatience of others. *Journeys* is a fact-based play about two asylum seekers who were refused asylum, locked up and detained despite experiencing rape, torture and imprisonment in their own country. *Motherland* reveals the extremely shocking and distressing experiences of women and children in the notorious Yarl's Wood detention centre. One woman, Saron, who was detained there asked to make a phone call and was told, 'This is not a prison, this is immigration detention. If you were in prison, you could call.' Lydia Besong's play *How I Became An Asylum Seeker* describes her experiences here after she left Cameroon, where she had been tortured for her political activities.

As I write, an exhibition about global urban refugees is about to go on display at St Pancras International Station. I hope people stop and look at it, in between getting their tickets for pleasure trips to Paris and business trips to Brussels and doing luxury shopping at L. K. Bennett and picking up cakes at Konditor & Cook patisserie and buying face cream from Neal's Yard Remedies for 30 pounds. It's funded by the European Commission's Humanitarian Aid and Civil Protection Department in partnership with the International Rescue Committee and features beautiful, dark-lit photographs by Andrew McConnell and the testimonies of the refugees who posed for him all over the world. In the testimonies, a woman from Haiti who was displaced by the 2010 earthquake was raped in the survivors' camp. A man who'd been a Pakistani human rights lawyer was targeted for assassination by extremists. A man from the Democratic Republic of Congo was targeted by rebels after he spoke out against the war between the government and militias. A man from Syria fled after his house was surrounded by snipers who killed four of his neighbours and his brother; he's pictured with his sons, who are in jeans and T-shirts, and two women in full black cover-all coats and black veils with a slit to see out of. One man from the Democratic Republic of Congo describes how rebels 'systematically raped the women'. Eight men raped his daughter and his wife was also raped. A woman from the Congo worked for a human rights association until rebels came to the village and raped the women. She says, 'When they left, the army came and did the same.' When she wrote a report on it, she was beaten by three soldiers. A month later, six soldiers came to her house, taped her mouth shut, tied her to the bed and raped her. She fled to Burundi, then Bangkok, where she applied for refugee status and was refused.

Although women do not make up even a quarter of McConnell's subjects, men's sexual violence runs through all their testimonies and is also the great unspoken, or half-spoken, or secretly spoken, in my classes. Admissions are made to me by students in private, confidentially, anonymously, as they have been by friends, relatives and colleagues all my life. Male sexual violence against women is a secret we all keep. In the world, as in the UK, it is endemic, yet women victims are disbelieved and male perpetrators are excused.

Women for Refugee Women undertook research recently which revealed the extent to which women asylum seekers had been attacked and victimized in such a way. The report, *Refused*, was based on the experiences of 72 women who'd applied for asylum in the UK.[17] Almost all had been refused asylum—in fact, nearly three-quarters of all women asylum seekers were turned away by the Home Office in 2010. In the study, nearly half of the refused women were made destitute and a quarter were put in detention centres. Further findings of the research were as follows:

> Of 72 women asylum seekers,
>
> - 49 per cent had experienced arrest or imprisonment in their home countries. One woman said, 'I was held in captivity. The actions I went through were degrading and inhuman.'
> - 52 per cent had experienced violence from soldiers, police or prison guards.
> - 32 per cent had been raped by soldiers, police or prison guards.

17 Kamena Dorling, Marchu Girma and Natasha Walter, *Refused: The Experiences of Women Denied Asylum in the UK* (London: Women for Refugee Women, 2012). Available at: http://www.refugeewomen.com/images/-refused.pdf (last accessed on 8 January 2014).

- 21 per cent had been raped by their husband, a family member or someone else.
- 48 per cent in total had been raped.
- Others were fleeing forced marriage, forced prostitution and female genital mutilation.

Of the 72 women, 70 disclosed the initial outcome of their asylum application:

- 67 of these 70 women had been refused asylum.
- 75 per cent of those refused said it was because they had not been believed.
- 67 per cent of those refused were made destitute.

Of the women who were made destitute,

- 96 per cent were relying on charities for food.
- 56 per cent were forced to sleep outside.
- 16 per cent had experienced sexual violence.
- 16 per cent had worked unpaid for food or shelter.

Natasha Walter writes in the report summary, 'Every year, hundreds of women who have survived rape and abuse experience destitution, detention and despair in this country.'[18] She is backed up by Debra Singer, policy and research manager at Asylum Aid: 'These are women fleeing

18 Cited in 'Women for Women Refugees'. Available at: http://www.refugee-women.com/index.php/resources/publications (last accessed on 8 January 2014).

unspeakable violence, yet they are routinely let down when they turn to the UK for help [. . .] women are routinely, arbitrarily disbelieved by [Home Office] officials when they explain what has happened to them.'[19]

The last of my notes is now transcribed, but for one. There's a piece of paper which doesn't have a name on it. It's dated from the session in the Bethnal Green centre when we looked through the lines of Shakespeare's sonnets and charted the intricate shifts of his emotions. At the top right of the sheet it says, 'Something you think about often.' In the middle, the student's sketched an airy diagram, a loose star of words. Death is in the middle, underlined and circled. Above it, growing out on a long stalk, is the word Reflection. On the left, The Mind. Below it, Love. At the bottom, in a little puff of blank space, is the word Regret. And on the right, at the end of a long line, as if running as far away from Death as it can get, is Memory.

19 Cited in ibid.

THE SIZE OF LOVE
Beatrice Tibahurira

One of my cherished memories is a trip I made when I was 11 with my mother, my aunt Lena and her daughter Ndinawe to visit my uncle John when he was still the English headmaster's houseboy. We travelled from Kabale to Mbarara. I had never been on a bus before. I was so excited that my brain must have captured the experience in such a way that I can still feel that excitement today.

My mother and her sister Lena were not only sisters but the best of friends. They put aside a day on a regular basis for meeting and talking for long hours. My mother and I would leave home very early in the morning as if going to dig a garden very far away. We would carry our lunch and any gifts for my aunt and her children. She would carry *akatebo*, a basket woven with reeds. In it would be foods like sweet potatoes, beans, peas, millet and sorghum bread and some greens like *dodo* (a spinach-like vegetable) or *eshwiga*, another vegetable.

I would carry *ekisisi* (calabash), a breakable container that is made by drying a certain type of mature pumpkin and taking out its insides and all the seeds to make it hollow. It is then used to store or carry drinks. Cut in half, it makes *orushare*, which is a cup or bowl used for drinking. We used *engata* to balance what we carried on our heads: *engata* is a small, round cushion made with reeds or dry banana leaves that are made into a circle, with another one or two knotted round. A smaller one for a child and a bigger one for an adult. It can even be made with a piece of cloth. It helps to balance any load to be carried on the head.

We would walk towards Kagarama, my aunt's village. We never used the road. We took connecting paths though the hills from Rwenzori through Akembwa to Rugarama and then Murwere, which is about halfway to Kagarama. Here we would meet my aunt and her children.

In the open fields, our mothers would choose a nice spot with grass like that of a well-kept garden or football pitch, where they would spread their cloths or mats to sit on. Traditionally, the Bakiga women wear dresses with gathers on the waist that go up to just below the knees, and throw a cloth over their shoulders. Usually, the dress and cloth are made from the same material.

From here, we could see across Kabale town, Muruhita, Nyakambu, Ndorwa, Rushoroza, Mwanjari and Makanga with Kabale hospital and the distinctive Administrative Offices and officers' residences. The view was spectacular. While our mothers sat and talked, we could sit, eat and play again and again until evening. We would exchange whatever gifts we had brought for each other like sugar, rice, dry mushrooms, smoked meat, fish or powdered milk. These were usually in small quantities, just to show love really. Our mothers would agree on when to meet again and then we would separate, reaching home at dusk.

I loved those meetings. There was so much love among us that as we said goodbye, we would be looking forward to the next meeting already. It was on such a day that they decided that for the next one we would meet at the UTC [Uganda Transport Corporation] bus park and go to Mbarara to visit Uncle John.

The UTC was at the end of Kabale town. Sadly it's not there any more as transport is now mostly privately run and the new park is at the other end of the town, near the market. But in those days, the heart of Kabale was the UTC. There were many UTC buses of green and yellow travelling to all parts of the country. Most travellers were Rwandans going to Buganda to look for manual work. Buganda was and still is the richest part of the country, with vast plantations of *matooke* bananas (green bananas, a staple food in Uganda) and coffee. We were one of the biggest suppliers of coffee to the world market. Kampala city is in Buganda, so it attracted and still attracts people from all parts of rural Uganda and from neighbouring Rwanda and Congo looking for a better life.

People like my mother and my aunt had no reason to travel in buses, so they never had done, let alone children like me and my cousin Ndinawe. I still remember the day we travelled as if it was yesterday. It was still dark when we woke up. My mother made fire on our *amahega* (fireplace) in our kitchen outside the house. She put on a big saucepan of water. After it was hot, she poured some in a small plastic basin and added cold water from a jerry can, then carried the basin of warm water to our makeshift bathroom behind the kitchen. First me, then my father and lastly she had a bath. An oil lantern was hanging on a nail in the bathroom. We had breakfast of a cup of tea and one sweet potato each. They tied our luggage on the carrier of my father's bicycle, then the three of us walked to the UTC. My Aunt Lena and Ndinawe were there before us, even though they lived further away from town.

The bus park was very busy. Women brought steaming pots of food to sell to travellers. They carried them in *entemere* (big, round baskets), balanced on their heads with *engata*. I knew some of the women who did this business because they were from my village. One of them, Nyinabushishire, was there that morning. She asked my mother where we were going and my mother told her that her brother, Uncle John, worked at Ntale school and we were going to visit him. She looked at us in awe and said that though she sold food to travellers, she never thought that she herself should ever travel, nor did she expect my mother to be travelling. I felt elevated above my village-mates because I knew Nyinabushishire would tell any-one who cared to listen that she had seen us get on a bus to Mbarara.

The four of us had sisal bags of foodstuffs including beans, peas and sorghum flour. Sorghum is a grain exclusive to Kabale district so it is the most common gift that people will take to others. Sisal or jute bags were the commonest way of carrying foodstuffs. My father, who had business at UTC, helped to get us two tickets for my mother and my aunt. On entering the bus, the conductor thought that Ndinawe was older than she was and should have paid. Our parents argued that she wasn't 14 yet. The conductor made her raise her right hand over her head and reach over to touch her left shoulder. This was supposed to show him whether she was over or under 14. She did and he was convinced that she was under, so she didn't need to pay. You see, we were the same age but she was taller than me.

The bus got so full that people were even sitting in the aisle on bags of sorghum or their bundles of clothes or on the floor. Others were standing with almost no breathing space. We were lucky as my father had arranged for my mother and my aunt to sit right behind the driver. Ndinawe and I were crammed between them and the driver's cabin, half sitting on their laps and half standing. I did not mind the discomfort. Being on a bus was reward enough.

The bus set off at eight. Being at a high altitude, our district was always very cold in the mornings with such thick mist that there was little visibility, if any. The bus was moving at a snail's pace to avoid collisions. At Nyakijumba, we left the lowland and started going uphill. On top of the hill, which is quite a long plateau, we were subdued, looking down onto the valleys of mist as if we were in the sky. There was a kind of euphoria on the bus. All quiet.

It wasn't until we reached Bukinda that the mist cleared. The bus, with its heavy burden, was moving slowly. The road, with its potholes, wasn't much help either. Here, we could see life around us. People going up the hills to dig, others taking their animals to graze, others riding their bicycles on the road or walking in either direction, many carrying their baskets of foodstuffs for sale. What struck me most was that people digging on the steep hillsides looked as if they may fall off. From my position on the bus, they seemed to be at 90 degrees to the hills.

We stopped once at a roadside market at Ntungamo. Here, people were roasting meat, maize, bananas, potatoes and more on open fires. They ran to the bus carrying baskets or waving sticks of these roasts and shouting 'Meat, meat, meat! Goat's meat fresh, cow's meat fatty, only one shilling!' or 'Maize, maize, maize! Fresh from the garden—all three for one shilling!' Things were cheap then. My mother bought us six cobs of maize for two shillings.

A journey which takes about two and a half hours today, took us six. We arrived at Mbarare UTC at 2 p.m. My uncle John and his wife Theresa were waiting for us. They tied the bags we had on the carrier of Uncle John's bicycle and we all walked to Ntale school. It is about half a mile from Mbarara town.

Uncle John and Theresa's home was one of the two rooms that made up the Boys' Quarters for the headmaster's residence. It was such a small room that I was worried we might not fit in, but we did. We stayed there for four days.

There is a saying of the Bakiga that 'It is people's hearts and people's feelings that fail to fit in a house.' That saying chimed so well with this visit. Its meaning is that people who care for each other will fit into any space available to them, however small it may be.

BIBLIOGRAPHY

ARBABZADEH, Nushin (ed.). *From Outside In: Refugees and British Society; An Anthology of Writings by Refugees on Britain and Britishness*. London: Arcadia Books, 2006.

BIDISHA. Introduction to *Big Writing for a Small World*. London: English PEN, 2012, p. 3.

BROCK, Lothar, Hans-Henrik Holm, Georg Sørensen and Michael Stohl. *Fragile States: War and Conflict in the Modern World*. Cambridge: Polity, 2012.

DIXON, Liz, Josie Harvey, Ron Thompson and Sarah Williamson. 'Practical Teaching' in James Avis, Roy Fisher and Ron Thompson (eds), *Teaching in Lifelong Learning: A Guide to Theory and Practice*. Maidenhead: McGraw-Hill International, 2009, pp. 119–42.

FRIEDMAN, Edie, and Reva Klein. *Reluctant Refuge: The Story of Asylum in Britain*. London: British Library, 2008.

RAMAN, Maneka, Cosh Omar, Vesna Maric, Kisti Joshi, Zlatko Pranjic, Nimer Rashed, Anita Sethi, Xenia Crockett, Nina Joshi, Toni Jackson, Mimi Chan-Choong, Cliff Walker, Ali Sheikholeslami, Marek Kazmierski, Jade Amoli-Jackson and Charmaine Joshua. *From There to Here: Sixteen True Tales of Immigration to Britain*. London: Penguin, 2007.

MOOREHEAD, Caroline. *Human Cargo: A Journey among Refugees*. London: Vintage, 2006.

SHERLOCK, Maeve. Foreword to Edie Friedman and Reva Klein, *Reluctant Refuge: The Story of Asylum in Britain*. London: British Library, 2008, pp. ix–x.

SMITH, Heather, and Mark K. Smith. *The Art of Helping Others: Being Around, Being There, Being Wise*. London: Jessica Kingsley, 2008.

WHITTAKER, David J. *Asylum Seekers and Refugees in the Contemporary World*. London: Routledge, 2006.

WINDER, Robert. *Bloody Foreigners: The Story of Immigration to Britain*. London: Little, Brown and Co., 2004.